Climate-Induced Innovation

Manuela Coromaldi · Sabrina Auci
Editors

Climate-Induced Innovation

Mitigation and Adaptation to Climate Change

palgrave
macmillan

Editors
Manuela Coromaldi
Department of Economics
University of Rome Niccolò Cusano
Rome, Italy

Sabrina Auci
Department of Political Science
and International Relations
University of Palermo
Palermo, Italy

ISBN 978-3-031-01329-4 ISBN 978-3-031-01330-0 (eBook)
https://doi.org/10.1007/978-3-031-01330-0

This Palgrave Macmillan imprint is published by the registered company Springer Nature Switzerland AG
The registered company address is: Gewerbestrasse 11, 6330 Cham, Switzerland

Foreword

'The modern world stands in need of biological renewal.' The words of Sir Muhammad Iqbal from 1938 remain valid. Iqbal was a poet and philosopher, a Muslim well aware of the developments of science in his day. But neither then, nor now is such a way of thinking widespread. The dominant mode of thought remains economic, and the authors of this book have carefully analysed the dynamics of their subject. The IPCC has produced another compendious analysis of facts and the trends to destruction which COP 26 in 2021 has failed to combat. In contrast to matters at COP 21 which in 2015 produced the Paris Agreement, adopted by 196 parties (countries) on 12th December 2015, the Glasgow meeting was overshadowed by the unbelievable statements of Boris Johnson, whose self-aggrandising tendencies have led to Brexit and to the subsequent diminished state of the United Kingdom on the world stage.

The Glasgow Climate Pact, signed by 120 countries on 13th December 2021, aims to limit rise in temperature to 1.5 degrees. But what is the point of that when the world is merely asked to phase down (a meaningless neologism) coal combustion and to stop subsidising fossil fuels? Where is there any evidence that the leader of any coal producing country has stated that this process of 'phasing down' (normally, phasing out) has begun? Where is there any statement from Australia, India or China at the top level of government that this matter is causing any action?

These treaties are supposed to be legally binding on the signatories, but it is not apparent that any of the 196 signatories to the Paris Agreement has initiated any legal proceedings to ensure compliance by anyone. British policy on 'the environment' is not at all exemplary. The fact is that in English law there is no right to a view. Thus, the idea of beauty in land use including planning decisions is excluded. The unimportance of the environment is so fundamental that when a leak in water supply pipes occurs in London, it may be days before it is repaired; with the loss of huge amounts of purified water and the consequent wasting of that water as it enters the sewerage. Floodwaters in Britain can destroy houses and be left stagnant for considerable periods, because government, central and local, is not organised effectively. Loss of power supply through severe storms in early 2022 took many days to overcome: for the same reasons of poor management and non-thinking.

The University of Birmingham has reported (March 7th 2022) that common house plants can improve the quality of air indoors. 'During a series of experiments monitoring common houseplants exposed to nitrogen dioxide (NO_2)—a common pollutant—researchers calculated that in some conditions, the plants could be able to reduce NO_2 by as much as 20 per cent.' But the actual paper makes clear that this work is related to a mere assertion by the government; not a fact achieved and evident from results corroborating the research. 'The UK government has set aside £255 million in the form of "the NO_2 plan", specifically implementing mitigation measures to reduce roadside emissions such as bus retrofits, clean air zones, traffic signal improvements and the phase out of diesel cars by 2040.'

These and similar analyses are not novel. What is astonishing is that the standing Royal Commission on Environmental Pollution from 1970 to 2011 did surveys of such problems which, in 2011, the Coalition Government ended as a cost-cutting exercise. One of the most obvious examples of the dominance of economics, this excellent mechanism for analysing environmental problems was closed for allegedly economic reasons. The ministerial statement suggested that the standing Royal Commission had merely raised awareness and was superfluous because there were now many available sources of information. With such marvellous insight, David Cameron went on to hold an undesirable referendum in 2016, in which he argued badly the case for remaining in the EU, and created many problems which have not even yet manifested their full force. The referendum was, legally, only advisory. Cameron's weakness in resigning caused it to appear to be decisive.

With such a mentality, no government—and Britain is merely a striking example of bad habits—can produce appropriate change in the foreseeable future. To say that this or that is a goal in 2040 or 2050 is to talk insincerely. No-one said in 2014, when Russia annexed Crimea, that in 2022 Russia would invade Ukraine and seek to absorb the identity of that independent, sovereign state as if it were merely a geographical element of Russia. No-one developed a policy of forward defence for Western Europe. So now, no-one in the British government appears to have the least interest in accelerating anti-pollution measures for air, water, land; or any interest in electric vehicles; or in the retrofitting of housing with insulation; or in providing subsidised heat pumps, solar panels, geothermal systems and windmills for the ordinary householder.

The British Government in the years 1970–2011 wasted all the reports from the standing Royal Commission on Environmental Pollution. The consumerism encouraged by Margaret Thatcher has proved simply that anyone can live selfishly, on deferred promises to pay for indulgence in sensation. The reality is that British industry was destroyed by Thatcher's economic policies with no alternative being devised, no adaptation to the challenges being faced, so that communities, individuals, skills, and hopes could be focused on change. And nothing very serious was done about environmental problems.

Environmental sustainability is a confusing idea when it is illustrated by a French plastic packet for cheese. This announces :- **EMBALLAGE RESPONSABLE**: La barquette de ce produit est fabriquée à partir de 30% de plastique recyclé, soit 24% de recyclage en moyenne dans l'emballage complet. Commerçants autrement

But in addition also, the packet says: BARQUETTE PLASTIQUE ET OPERCULE A JETER

And then, finally: CONSIGNE DE TRI POUVANT VARIER SELON VOTRE COMMUNE

The latest IPCC report may seem to displace responsibility from the 'commune' or the state to the individual. All individuals live in atomised societies with very weak unifying elements in our secular, confused world. Unless politics manifests responsible leaders, with effective policies, societies will only drift closer to rapids and waterfalls.

This book instead says that to mitigate climate change is also to adapt to it, and adaptation leads to innovation. That may be a statement of hope, but if one believes it, with sacrificial love for the world one may indeed redeem the lost time and save the future.

Lorigné, France

Michael Brett-Crowther
Editor
International Journal of Environmental Studies

References

de Bary, ed., Sources of Indian Tradition, vol II, 1958 (New York & London: Columbia University Press), p. 209

https://www.ipcc.ch/report/ar6/wg2/

https://unfccc.int/sites/default/files/english_paris_agreement.pdf

https://glasgowagreement.net/en/

Common houseplants can improve air quality indoors. University of Birmingham, press release. March 7 2022.

Gubb, C., Blanusa T., Griffiths. A., & Pfrang, C., 2022, Potted plants can remove the pollutant nitrogen dioxide indoors. Air Quality, Atmosphere & Health 15, 479–490.

https://www.gov.uk/government/organisations/department-for-environment-food-rural-affairs

Introduction

Global economic growth implies positive spillovers such as new knowledge and technological change, but also negative ones such as pollution, climate change, and biodiversity loss. This can be summarized by the long-standing debate about natural resources and environmental limits to growth and the ability to overcome them through human creativity. Climate change and innovation might at first glance seem to be two separate issues, but as argued by Nordhaus (2019) "The truth is that they are manifestations of the same fundamental phenomenon, which is a global externality or global public good. Both involve science and technology, and both involve the inability of private markets to provide an efficient allocation of resources". Therefore, solving the problem of climate change is a difficult task, it involves a wide variety of disciplines such as atmospheric chemistry and climate science, ecology, economics, political science, and so on. Moreover, given that it represents a global public "bad", it requires the design and the implementation of cooperative multinational policies that imply cooperation among nations even when individual nations enjoy only a small fraction of the benefits of their actions (Nordhaus, 2019).

In the coming decades, the world can expect to experience significant uncertainty due to problems and opportunities posed by the transition to becoming an environmentally sustainable society. Whether firms and institutions will be able to deal with these threats is contingent on their ability to adapt their practices, know-how, skills, and routines to the changing climate. Not surprisingly, this challenge largely depends on innovation. Scholars and decision-makers acknowledge that climate change and climate variability are one of the most significant societal, economic, and environmental threats humanity faces nowadays. A possible solution to avoid the negative consequences of climate change/variability can only come from new practices and technologies.

Therein, two broad technological domains can deal with climate change. On the one hand, climate change mitigation technologies aim to tackle the negative environmental impacts by reducing the negative environmental externalities of the production and distribution process. On the other hand, technological innovation can also be an important form of adaptation. It provides the necessary tools for people to adapt to a changing environment. It enhances the capacity to cope with natural hazards and provides adaptation strategies. Therefore, technologies for adaptation to climate change emerge as a response to the threats brought about by climate change/variability. In this context, mitigation technologies affect climate change by reducing the causes that generate it, while adaptation-related innovation increases resilience and does not directly affect climate change since its objective is to enhance firms' adaptive opportunities in a changing environment.

Almost all the research on green induced innovation focuses on technologies designed to reduce pollution. However, with regard to climate change, since it is already happening, innovation to reduce pollution is just as relevant as innovation to adapt to new climatic conditions. The process towards reducing greenhouse gas emissions seems to be too slow and long. Reducing emissions to a level that would completely prevent further climate change still seems to be lacking. For this reason, adaptation to climate change will be an undeniably significant part of any climate policy, and the development of new technologies has an important role to play in future adaptation strategies (Popp, 2019). So, technological progress may reduce the negative impact of human activities on climate change and, in the meanwhile, improve the adaptation capacity to cope with climate change. While mitigation actions are more related to the reduction of greenhouse gases' sources, adaptation entails bottom-up efforts that actors either put in place proactively or reactively to actual or expected climate effects.

The goal of this study is to produce a timely book that provides new insight on the relationship between climate change strategies and innovation for international readers and makes these environmental issues more accessible to post-graduate students, researchers, academics, social and economic scientists, institutional workers, and practitioners who are engaged in the field of the environment, innovation, and sustainable livelihood.

This book, thus, introduces an innovative approach to investigate the role of climate-induced innovation in the context of climate change mitigation technologies as well as climate change adaptation strategies. Indeed, this study is one of the first attempts of combining two different economic streams of literature. One is focused on the relationship between innovation and mitigation and, the other, less developed, on innovation as an adaptation strategy.

By offering new case studies, the contributors present new approaches and methods to analyse the effects of climate-induced innovation in climate change adaptation and mitigation.

Specifically, this book pursues its objectives by focusing on firms/regions located in European countries as well as on farmers placed in developing ones. Given that the sectors most affected by climate change are undoubtedly resource-based sectors such as agroforestry, water, animal husbandry, fisheries, and aquaculture, the case studies presented in this book stress how innovation and new technologies in the agricultural sector may represent a strategy to mitigate and adapt to climate change effects.

We believe European firms, operating in the agricultural sector, are suitable for our purposes as they allow us to follow the evolutionary dynamics, stimulated by climatic variability, leading to the production of new technological knowledge (e.g., The European Union's long-term strategy for agricultural research and innovation). Indeed, developing countries differ from high-income countries in terms of capacity to react to the climate change stimulus and ability to enable effective transformation processes. This happens mainly when additional investments for innovation are required. In fact, transformation and innovation are not low-hanging fruits. Several developing countries have very limited resources to invest to upgrade processes, technologies, products, and infrastructure to adapt to climate change. Similarly, most of them have scarce ability to finance or inadequate technical skills to develop new climate-proof production methods. This also leads to a reduced opportunity to develop new technological and formal knowledge.

The literature on innovation has provided evidence that these countries rely mainly on low-tech solutions. However, developing countries could be encouraged to adopt new technologies developed by high-income countries. For example, in the agricultural sector, which is among those most affected by climate change, it is found that even when the transfer of knowledge between developed and developing countries occurs, the adoption of new technologies by farmers remains low and policies such as extension services to support them are needed. On the other hand, developed countries are also vulnerable to climate change and this calls for climate actions within the European Union (EU) or other high-income countries, especially in the agriculture sector (EEA, 2019). Hence, we believe that it is paramount to develop ad hoc studies for developed countries and to fill the gap in the literature by extending the coverage of analyses to the EU as well. We hope, however, we have included topics that are both interesting and relevant for the analysis of climate change and innovation issues.

The organization of this book is based on four chapters. The first chapter is an introduction to and an overview of the two main issues addressed in the book: climate change and innovation economics. In this chapter some background on climate change and innovation economics in the context of mitigation technologies and adaptation strategies are provided. Chapter 2 shows an empirical application of the effect of the innovation generation process on firm efficiency in developed countries, regardless of its level of adoption. This section illustrates the effect of climate-induced innovation on European farmers' technical efficiency. Patents are used as a good indicator of innovation in agricultural biotechnology and are introduced in the model to investigate the relationship between innovation and efficiency. The third chapter is devoted to calling attention to the difficulties in adopting new technologies in a developing country like Ghana. Specifically, based on the existing literature as well as on field observations and interviews, the analysis focuses on the issues hindering the adoption of innovations for sustainable cocoa farming. The last chapter provides comprehensive information on the technologies and practices known as climate-smart agriculture and their intersection with global climate change. More precisely, based on the theory and concepts of global adaptation and mitigation strategies, this chapter deepens the conceptual framework of climate-smart agriculture as well as provides a certain number of global case studies.

Therefore, focusing on the combination of adaptation and mitigation strategies, as this book does, can contribute to better understanding of the steps as well as the policies needed to support innovation activities and to favour the transition to an environmentally sustainable society.

References

Nordhaus, W. (2019). Climate change: The ultimate challenge for economics. American Economic Review, 109(6), 1991–2014.

Popp, D. (2019). Environmental policy and innovation: A decade of research. 860 National Bureau of Economic Research Working Paper Series (w25631).

Contents

List of Contributors

Asare Richard International Institute of Tropical Agriculture, Accra, Ghana

Auci Sabrina Department of Political Science and International Relations, University of Palermo, Palermo, Italy

Azadi Hossein Department of Economics and Rural Development, Gembloux Agro-Bio Tech, University of Liège, Gembloux, Belgium; Ghent, Belgium

Boadi Sylvester Afram Department of Geography and Resource Development, University of Ghana, Legon, Ghana

Bosselmann Aske Skovmand Department of Food and Resource Economics, University of Copenhagen, Frederiksberg, Denmark

Burkart Stefan Tropical Forages Program, The Alliance of Bioversity International and the International Center for Tropical Agriculture (CIAT), Cali, Colombia

Coromaldi Manuela Department of Economics, University of Rome Niccolò Cusano, Rome, Italy

Dogot Thomas Department of Economics and Rural Development, Gembloux Agro-Bio Tech, University of Liège, Gembloux, Belgium

Goli Imaneh Department of Economics, Agricultural Extension and Education, Tehran Science and Research Branch, Islamic Azad University, Tehran, Iran

Lebailly Philippe Department of Economics and Rural Development, Gembloux Agro-Bio Tech, University of Liège, Gembloux, Belgium

Miceikienė Astrida Agriculture Academy, Vytautas Magnus University, Kaunas distr, Lithuania

Moghaddam Saghi Movahhed Faculty of Environmental Sciences, Czech University of Life Sciences Prague, Prague, Czech Republic

Olwig Mette Fog Department of Social Sciences and Business, Roskilde University, Roskilde, Denmark

Owusu Kwadwo Department of Geography and Resource Development, University of Ghana, Legon, Ghana

Siamian Narges Faculty of Natural Resources and Environment, Science and Research Branch, Department of Environmental Science, Islamic Azad University, Tehran, Iran

Teklemariam Dereje Department of Management, Debre Berhan University, Debre Berhan, Ethiopia

Van Passel Steven Department of Engineering Management, University of Antwerp, Antwerp, Belgium

Abbreviations

CA	Conservation Agriculture
CO2	Carbon dioxide
CRA	Climate-Resistant Agriculture
CSA	Climate-Smart Agriculture
EIs	Environmental Innovations
EPO	European Patent Office
EU	European Union
FADN	Farm Accountancy Data Network
FAO	Food and Agriculture Organization of the United Nations
GHG	Greenhouse Gases
ICT	Information Communication Technology
ICTSD	International Centre for Trade and Sustainable Development
OECD	Organisation for Economic Co-operation and Development
PATSTAT	Worldwide Patent Statistical Database
PCA	Principal Component Analysis
R&D	Research and Development
SFA	Stochastic Frontier Analysis
SHG	Self-Help Group
SOC	Soil Organic Carbon
SQI	Soil Quality Indices
UNEP	United Nations Environment Programme
VCRMC	Village Climate Risk Management Committee
VSA	Vulnerable-Smart Agriculture
WHO	World Health Organization

List of Figures

List of Tables

CHAPTER 1

A Short Survey on Climate Change and Environmental Innovations

Manuela Coromaldi and Sabrina Auci

Abstract Climate change is and will be in the coming years one of the major challenges facing the world. The best strategy to cope with climate anomalies seems to be fostering the ability to innovate and find technological solutions. Therefore, understanding the relationship between the stimuli brought about by climate variability and the propensity to innovate is of paramount importance. To this end, this chapter provides some background on climate change and innovation economics and then focuses on climate-induced innovation in the context of mitigation technologies and adaptation strategies.

M. Coromaldi (✉)
Department of Economics, University of Rome Niccolò Cusano, Rome, Italy
e-mail: manuela.coromaldi@unicusano.it

S. Auci
Department of Political Science and International Relations, University of Palermo, Palermo, Italy
e-mail: sabrina.auci@unipa.it

M. Coromaldi and S. Auci (eds.), *Climate-Induced Innovation*,
https://doi.org/10.1007/978-3-031-01330-0_1

Keywords Climate change · Adaptation · Mitigation · Climate-induced innovation · Environmental innovation

1.1 Introduction

Climate change is now recognized as a global challenge, the effects of which manifest themselves locally and may differ from country to country. Given the need to manage risks from climate change, this chapter begins by reviewing the literature on environmental innovations and climate-induced innovations for supporting adaptation and mitigation strategies. Limiting the emission of greenhouse gases (GHGs) emitted by human activities and promoting adaptation to the unavoidable effects of climate change can make these impacts less severe and countries more climate resilient.

Addressing climate change means pursuing both mitigation and adaptation since they represent the two sides of the same coin. Methods and technologies that limit GHG emissions and manage the negative impacts of climate change do already exist. There are several common factors underlying adaptation and mitigation reactions such as effective institutions and governance, innovation and investments in environmentally sound technologies, and infrastructure. Specifically, while investments in low-carbon and carbon–neutral energy technologies may mitigate the emissions of GHGs, investments in new technologies for adaptation may increase the resilience of human systems (IPCC 2014a).

Technological improvements have played a relevant role in reducing environmental pressure from production and consumption (Popp et al. 2010). In this way, the decoupling between economic growth and environmental degradation could be achieved and a win–win situation may emerge when environmental quality and economic growth coexist (Barbieri et al. 2016). Focusing only on environmental induced innovation to mitigate climate change may not be sufficient, since there exist inter-relationships between adaptation and mitigation. Mitigation efforts can foster adaptive capacity by eliminating market failures and distortions and vice versa since adaptation may have positive and negative effects on mitigation actions. As a consequence, climate policy should implement a portfolio of different adaptation and mitigation actions integrated into a multiple societal objectives approach (Klein et al. 2007; IPCC 2014b; Popp 2019).

Environmental innovations (EIs) have assumed a relevant role in the actual policy debate, especially within the European Union (EU). In the framework of European climate policy, EU actions aim to mitigate and adapt to climate change effects. From the mitigation point of view, the EU supports the innovation in the use of renewable energy, such as wind, solar, hydro, and biomass, to improve energy efficiency, while on the adaptation actions, the strategy proposed is to improve knowledge, manage uncertainty, and make adaptation actions systematic.

Thus, considerable literature has examined environmental innovation focusing on the relationship between environmental policy and innovation. Among the most comprehensive reviews of this literature are four interesting surveys: Popp et al. (2010), Barbieri et al. (2016), Popp (2019), and Aldieri et al. (2019). All these reviews focus mainly on eco-friendly innovations to mitigate the impacts of climate change. This chapter contributes to the literature by focusing on climate-induced innovation within the broader stream of environmental innovations. Specifically, the chapter highlights the technological innovation role in future mitigation and adaptation strategies.

The structure of the chapter is as follows. In Sect. 1.2, climate change challenges and economic impacts are explored. Section 1.3 and Sect. 1.4 analyze environmental innovation and climate-induced innovation literature, respectively.

1.2 Climate Change Challenges and Economic Impacts

Climate change is acknowledged to be one of the major externalities. It is considered the mother of all externalities. This means it has a life span of several decades and is probably even longer and more uncertain than any other environmental problem. It is a particularly spiny externality because it is a global phenomenon that shows marked local consequences and manifests itself in heterogeneous ways across regions and sectors (IPCC 2014b).

Recent findings have shown that the increasing variability of weather and climate parameters and the frequency of extreme weather events are likely to intensify the incidence of environmental disasters (IPCC 2018a) and to lead to the depletion of natural resources endangering their global supply, especially for climate-sensitive sectors such as agroforestry, water, animals breeding, fishing and aquaculture, tourism, etc. (IPCC 2014b; Hernández-Delgado 2015; Stevanovic et al. 2016; EEA 2019).

Estimating the economic impact of future climate change is a very difficult task because of all the uncertainties associated with the global warming phenomenon. The impact projections that have been carried out so far converge on one point, namely that the impacts of climate change are non-linear and cumulative (IPCC 2014a, 2018a). The maximum damages are likely to be most concentrated in low-income and tropical regions where rain-fed agriculture is prevalent such as tropical Africa and Latin America. Also, coastal states and the Indian subcontinent could be heavily affected (Nordhaus 2019). In the IPCC's 2018a report on 1.5 °C (IPCC 2018a), the authors suggest that a warming of just 2 °C would be highly detrimental to both human and natural systems.

Through the interaction among various events, such as demographic growth, increased globalization and urbanization, climate change will likely pose huge challenges for developed as well as developing countries. The latter group of countries is and will continue to be one of those most severely affected by enduring climate changes. In the last decades, Africa, for example, experienced more erratic precipitation, changing patterns of rainfall, increasing average temperatures, changes in water supply and ongoing sea-level rise. All this happened in regions that already suffer from aridity, recurring drought, and water scarcity. Also in developed countries, climate change is expected to affect water resources that are already badly exploited by humans. For example, the unsustainable irrigation practices, the high rates of human water consumption and the construction of dams are likely to exacerbate this situation. Moreover, in countries where population and most economic activities are located in coastal areas, the sea-level rise is likely to increase their vulnerability as they are exposed to inundation and the rising salinity of the soil.

Climate change is also expected to impact biodiversity that has declined and continues to do so at a high pace because of the anthropic activities.[1] All ecosystems (marine, terrestrial, and freshwater) are affected by the changes in precipitation, seasonality, storm intensity, and more. For example, as a response to the changing of climatic parameters about half of the species (mainly animals), on which there were data,

[1] The loss of biodiversity, in turn, has huge consequences for climate change, as large amounts of carbon are locked up in animal life and vegetation (Dasgupta 2021).

have shifted toward the poles. Furthermore, marine species distribution change is faster than terrestrial one (Lovejoy and Hannah 2019). Climate change contributes to rapid and large-scale changes, with significant consequences for ecosystems. It can trigger mega-fires (as happened in Australia in late 2019 and early 2020) and lead to extinctions caused by droughts, floods, and hurricanes. It can also promote pest and pathogen outbreaks, although the study of this relationship is rather complex (Jactel, Koricheva, and Castagneyrol 2019). The changing climate is also altering marine biomes. The ocean, with its capability to absorb CO2 and heat, plays a crucial role. It has absorbed 93% of the additional heat that exists due to the greenhouse effect, and about 30% of the CO2 generated by human activities. This absorption has led to a rise in sea level, a reduction in the extent of sea ice, and a sudden drop in ocean pH. As a result, among other things, this has contributed to the threat to coral reefs, which, despite occupying only 0.1% of the Earth's surface, are home to around 25% of known marine organisms (Hoegh-Guldberg et al., 2019). [2]

The change of the species distribution due to rising temperatures also negatively affects human health. The migration of disease vectors such as mosquitoes is very likely to increase cases of mosquito-borne infectious diseases such as malaria (Caminade et. 2014). Malaria will become more widespread and will affect new territories because higher temperatures reduce the incubation period, spread the range of malaria-carrying mosquitoes, and will increase their abundance. Furthermore, climate change patterns also affect water availability along with water governance and management issues. In addition to water scarcity, water quality is also relevant. This is adversely affected by waterborne pathogens and consequently heavily impacting on human health, which depends on clean water (Ahmed et al. 2020). According to the WHO (2016), half of the world's population will suffer from water stress conditions by 2025 and at least 2 billion people around the world are forced to consume contaminated water from sewers for drinking, which leads to the transfer of diseases such as cholera, typhoid, dysentery, and polio. Poor water

[2] As well as changing the distribution of species on land and in the seas and altering ecosystems, climate change has also left its mark on the genomes of organisms. In particular, selection for genes that allow organisms to survive at higher temperatures has been identified such as in the American pika, a small relative of rabbits and hares (Lemay et al. 2013) or in oaks (Quercus lobata) (Sork et al. 2016).

quality means more expenditure on health, as people are more likely to fall ill and incur medical costs and are less able to remain economically productive.

Similarly, air quality is strongly dependent on weather and is therefore sensitive to climate change which is the main cause of the increase in the frequency of stagnation episodes over the northern continents in the mid-latitudes. This increase in stagnation reflects the weakening of the general circulation and a northward shift of mid-latitude cyclones, thus decreasing the frequency of cold fronts that are the main ventilation mechanism for eastern North America, Europe, and eastern Asia (Jacob and Winner 2009). So, meteorological variables such as temperature, humidity, wind speed, and direction play important roles in determining patterns of air quality over multiple scales in time and space. There is a growing consensus that the development of strategies to control future levels of key health pollutants such as ozone and fine particles (particulate matter, PM2.5) should include an assessment of potential future climatic conditions and their possible influence on the achievement of air quality objectives (Kinney 2008). Air quality is also of relevance to human health. For example, increased CO2 concentration or more intense and frequent sandstorms in desert areas could deteriorate air quality increasing allergic reactions and lung diseases.

Directly related to human health is also food production, which will be increasingly threatened by erratic precipitation, droughts, and floods, thus affecting basic human needs and jeopardizing food security. Thus, food security is sustained by well-functioning food systems, which are a set of dynamic complex inter-actions between and within bio-geophysical and human environments. They encompass a range of activities (food production; food processing, packaging, and distribution; food conservation; food retailing and consumption), which result in a number of related outcomes, some contributing to food security (i.e., food availability, food access, and food utilization) and others addressing environmental and other social well-being issues (Smith 2013). Food production from agriculture in particular is strongly reliant on temperature and rainfall and therefore sensitive to climate change. Although some regions have been experiencing productivity gains, on average agriculture and human welfare will be negatively impacted by climate change (Nelson et al. 2009). Increases in aridity and changes in seasonal patterns can halve agricultural yields deteriorating food availability and quality. In a recent study, Ray et al. (2019) found that climate change has already affected global food production. Authors estimated the potential impact of observed climate change on the yields of the top ten global crops: barley, cassava, maize, oil palm, rapeseed, rice, sorghum, soybean, sugarcane, and wheat. What emerges from the analysis is that the globally driven climate change impact on yields of different crops ranges from -13.4% (oil palm) to 3.5% (soybean) and that such impacts are largely negative in Europe, southern Africa, and Australia, but generally positive in Latin America. In Asia and North and Central America, the impacts are mixed.

Thus, one of the main challenges, humanity should address in the twenty-first century is to provide sustainable nutrition for nine to ten billion people by 2050, while simultaneously reducing environmental burdens (e.g., greenhouse gas (GHG) emissions, biodiversity loss, land-use change, and loss of ecosystem services). It, therefore, appears to be necessary to enhance the production potential of crops as well as to improve the resilience of food production to future environmental change largely through the use of new technologies and investment in research.

Urgent adaptation measures such as changes in crop varieties, fertilizers, and irrigation practices are therefore needed. The development of new crop varieties that can adapt to emerging conditions should be encouraged. Crops that need less water and can withstand higher levels of salinity should be developed and introduced on a large scale.

All these climate-related factors listed above can be better handled through innovative solutions. Innovation can be driven not only by finding solutions to mitigate the effects of climate change, but also by the development of strategies to cope with its immediate effects. Adaptation to new climate parameters means inventing new solutions to offset the negative effects of the climate. As a result, the impacts of climate change and variability on economic and social systems will be space-varying with effects that translate into different responses as a function of socio-economic heterogeneity (ECONADPT 2016; Zilberman et al. 2018) and dissimilar adaptive capacity (Vanschoenwinkela et al. 2016). Therefore, policymakers and scholars concur that the transition toward low-emission and sustainable societies, which Europe, as well as other countries, will have to enhance over the coming decades, revolves greatly around the development and adoption of environmentally sound technologies (Jaffe et al. 2005; Popp et al. 2010; Ahman et al. 2018), enabling climate change adaptation and mitigation.

To this end, in the next section, we present a brief review of the literature on environmental innovation to provide a better understanding of its drivers as well as its economic and environmental effects.

1.3 Environmental Innovation: Determinants, Economic, and Environmental Effects

In the innovation literature, economic risk and uncertainty are the main determinants of innovative activity (Dosi 1988; Kline and Rosenberg 2010). As underlined by Popp et al. (2010), technological improvements may reduce the environmental pressure of human activities when are aimed to boost economic growth. A criticism of this literature is that human inventive activity cannot indefinitely increase global production without having negative effects on economic stability. Moreover, this literature has considered economic growth as a necessary tool to finance the innovation to reduce carbon emissions to zero without asking if the same economic growth is appropriate for measuring sustainable development (Dasgupta 2021).

By improving environmental quality and decreasing environmental pressure, technological innovation allows a society to meet its environmental targets. EIs are different from other technological innovations. Stimulating environmental innovations means improving the innovation intensity of an economy and the environmental efficiency of a production process. Thus, the positive effects on the environment may be counterbalanced with negative effects due to the production structure, i.e., the small size of firms may reduce the ability to invest and innovate and thus increase the loss in firm productivity and competitiveness (Aldieri et al. 2019; Arbolino et al. 2018). Since environmental regulations can lead to low levels of firm productivity, Palmer et al. (1995) have criticized the imposition of strict standards.

Barbieri et al. (2016), in their survey on the EI literature, define the "environmental innovation" notion as all those product or production process innovations that reduce environmental risk, pollution, and other negative impacts of resource use. In this stream of literature, the analyses focus on four main topics which are the *determinants*, *economic effects*, *environmental effects*, and *policy inducement* of EIs.

As regards the *determinants of EI adoption*, Rennings (2000) highlights that they are characterized by the "double externality" hypothesis.

This means that EIs, at the same time, may reduce negative environmental externalities and enhance positive knowledge externalities. Indeed, knowledge spillovers produced by firms that develop and/or adopt innovations may be beneficial to other firms. Thus, among the determinants of EIs, four groups of drivers can be distinguished: ***market-pull***, ***technology-push***, ***firm-specific factors*** and ***regulation*** (Horbach 2008; Horbach et al. 2012; for a review see Ghisetti and Pontoni 2015, and Barbieri et al. 2016). The firm choice of protecting the environment is driven by the market conditions (***market-pull***) such as demand for more eco-products, consumer preferences for environmentally friendly goods, and so on. Also, technological factors (***technology-push***), as well as market conditions, are important to stimulate EI adoption. These factors depend on the knowledge-capital endowment of firms as well as organizational and managerial capabilities. In addition, R&D investments or activities may increase the knowledge and skills of employees and as a consequence, this may enhance firm productivity. As regards the ***firm-specific factors***, the firm innovative capability may be influenced by several firm characteristics, such as size, location, sector, and age. Environmental innovations are mainly regulation-driven (***regulation***) and are characterized by the so-called "regulatory (policy) push/pull effect". This means that the legislation may stimulate EIs through both the supply side (push) and the demand side (pull) (Rennings 2000). By modifying the relative production factor prices and imposing compulsory rules, regulation incentivizes EIs in each phase of the innovation process (invention, adoption, and diffusion) (Popp 2005). In addition to the regulatory effect, EIs are also affected by corporate social and environmental responsibility as investigated by Ghisetti and Quatraro (2013). Their analysis confirms that firm innovation activity may be induced endogenously in a context characterized by a weak environmental regulatory framework.

The analysis of *EI economic effects* is relevant for political decision-making. In an ex-post policy evaluation, these effects include both the direct benefits of EI policy stimuli and those for the society in reducing the environmental externalities. Furthermore, analyzing the relationship between EI and economic performance may be relevant for the choice of the appropriate policy tools to be implemented. Identifying which are the more suitable ones allows aligning two aims in potential conflicts such as economic sustainability and profit maximization (Aldieri et al. 2019). As underlined by Porter and Van der Linde (1995), EIs stimulated by regulation are more likely to have positive impacts on the long-term performance such as firm profits rather than on short-term measures as productivity, international competitiveness, and so on. In the Aldieri et al. (2019) review, they confirmed that policies supporting EIs should be warranted because well-designed environmental policies could boost economic growth and protect the environment.

Among the studies on *environmental effects* of EIs, Jaffe et al. (2002) underlined how technological change is essential to achieve environmental sustainability. However, Barbieri et al. (2016) point out that two considerations may be drawn: first, the mechanism through which innovation exerts its effect on the environment is not unique and second, to reduce the negative environmental impact, innovation alone is not sufficient. Specifically, the mechanism through which innovation can affect environmental performance is threefold. First, EIs may indirectly affect variables relevant to improving environmental performance. Mazzanti and Zoboli (2009), considering 29 sectors in Italy and 6 pollutants over the 1991–2001 period, found that environmental innovation affects indirectly labor productivity. Second, in the presence of spatial spillover effects, EIs influence agents' choices in neighboring areas and regions. Analogous results may be found in Costantini et al. (2013)' analysis that considers the role of innovation, regional environmental spillovers, and environmental policies. They found that innovation and environmental spillovers can drive regional and sector-specific environmental outcomes. Thus, the authors conclude that the role of spillover is even more crucial than that of innovation in defining environmental performance. Third, EIs may determine environmental and investment decisions through the presence of cross-sectorial spillovers. Innovations may spread widely at the sector level. Dopfer (2012) showed how cross-sectorial spillovers incentivize the adoption of innovations, contributing to increasing potential environmental benefits.

Finally, the *role of policy* to induce environmentally friendly innovations is widely studied in the EI literature (Barbieri et al. 2016). Stringent environmental regulations may incentivize the development of cleaner technologies since R&D expenditure follows the profit-maximization hypothesis. The empirical literature on the effect of policy on environmental innovation is based on the theoretical background (the induced innovation assumption) developed by Hicks (1932), Acemoglu (2002), and Acemoglu et al. (2012). Reinforced by the hypothesis of Porter (1991) and Porter and Van der Linde (1995), a well-designed policy framework allows firms to develop innovations and promote product and process technological change. Based on the so-called Porter Hypothesis (narrow, weak, or strong), environmental regulations stimulating innovations are able to promote competitiveness across firms and countries. In their review on induced innovation and Porter hypothesis, Ambec et al. (2013) show that innovation in clean technologies is incentivized by stricter environmental policies, and innovative response to policy usually happens quickly. Moreover, Aldieri et al. (2019) underline how, by focusing on pollution abatement, public policy strategies may address the research about the reduction of negative emissions favoring the sustainability of a territory. Using regulations and incentives as policy instruments to mitigate negative environmental externalities, policymakers may create new opportunities for the development of environmental innovations. When designing policies to address the impacts of climate change, EIs can help mitigate future greenhouse gas emissions or can be induced by the need to adapt to the adverse effects of climate change. The importance of EIs, along with actions to tackle the negative consequences of climate change, is recognized by the United Nations, which has included them as targets in the 2030 Agenda for Sustainable Development and the Sustainable Development Goals. Therefore, in the following section, we deepen the analysis of climate-induced innovations by discussing the innovation that comes from the need to mitigate or adapt to climate change.

1.4 Climate-Induced Innovation: Mitigation Technologies and Adaptation Strategies

In the previous section, the literature related to the development and adoption of climate-induced innovation to address weather and climate variability was reviewed. Before discussing the two aspects of climate-induced innovation, namely generated by the need to mitigate the effects of climate change and arising as a matter of adaptation to climate variability, we attempt to define these two terms "adaptation" and "mitigation". In the climate change debate, climate mitigation means any action that aims to eliminate or permanently reduce the long-term risk and hazard of climate change to human life.[3] According to the Intergovernmental Panel on Climate Change mitigation is defined as: "An anthropogenic intervention to reduce the sources or enhance the sinks of greenhouse gases". Climate adaptation refers to the "Adjustment in natural or human systems in response to actual or expected climatic stimuli or their effects, which moderates harm or exploits beneficial opportunities" (IPCC 2018b). Thus, it refers to the ability of a system to adapt to climate variability and extreme weather events in order to moderate potential damage.

The level of climate change impacts is determined by adaptation and mitigation efforts, operating at different spatial and temporal scales (Smith et al. 2001; IPCC 2007). That is, system resilience can be fostered both by risk mitigation activities undertaken before the disaster and by response activities after the event. Mitigation has global benefits, although ancillary benefits could be achieved at the local level and must involve a sufficient number of large GHG emitters to exclude leakage. Adaptation, on the other hand, typically works at the scale of an affected system, which is mostly local or at most regional.[4] The benefits of mitigation undertaken today will be revealed in the long run, due to the long residence time of greenhouse gases in the atmosphere,[5] while many adaptation measures would be effective immediately and produce benefits by reducing vulnerability to climate variability.

An integrated portfolio of actions is needed, ranging from avoiding emissions (mitigation) to coping with impacts (adaptation). However, the empirical literature seems to have expressed no great interest in exploring the interrelationship between adaptation and mitigation. While acknowledging the dual necessity of adaptation and mitigation, there is little literature that recognizes the need to explore trade-offs and synergies between the two responses. Research on adaptation and mitigation has

[3] Mitigation refers to actions or policies that reduce emissions of greenhouse gases (such as carbon dioxide [CO2], methane [CH4] and nitrous oxide [N2O]) that can cause global warming, or measures that directly aim to absorb these gases from the atmosphere (e.g., reforestation).

[4] Although some adaptation could result in spillovers across national boundaries, for example by changing international commodity prices in agricultural or forestry product markets.

[5] Actually, ancillary benefits such as reductions in air pollution are possible in the short term.

been so far rather unconnected, involving largely different communities of scholars who have adopted different approaches to explore the two responses separately. Focusing on climate-induced innovation, we try to fill the gap in the literature by analyzing the two sides of the same coin: innovation in terms of new mitigation technologies and innovative adaptation strategies.

Two main streams of literature are involved. First, the one that relies on those studies that investigate whether and to what extent environmental/climatic conditions affect innovation. Therein, the so-called *induced innovation* hypothesis has been explored extensively from different perspectives (for an overview of these studies see Popp et al. 2010). This posits that innovation is affected by the change in the relative price of production factors: i.e., it is introduced to reduce the usage of those factors that become more expensive (Hicks 1932). This hypothesis provided a solid background for several studies that, for example, explore the impact of energy prices and environmental regulations on the development of green technologies (see e.g., Newell et al. 1999; Popp 2002; Barbieri 2015).

As regards climate change mitigation technologies, one of the first studies on a global scale is the joint EPO-UNEP-ICTSD (2010) report on "Patents and clean energy technologies: bridging the gap between energy and policy", published in 2010. Using the European Patent Office (EPO)'s Worldwide Patent Statistical Database (PATSTAT), the report found that only six OECD countries (the US, Japan, Korea, France, Germany, and the UK) have filed climate change mitigation technology patents in the period 1980–2009. The analysis of Dechezleprêtre et al. (2011) confirms that innovation in climate change mitigation technologies was highly concentrated in Japan, Germany, and the US. Moreover, they found that, up to 1990, energy prices incentivized innovation in climate change mitigation technologies. After 1990, the role of environmental and climate policy has become predominant in inducing more innovation, with acceleration after the signing of the Kyoto Protocol in 1997. In addition, environmental policies encourage the international diffusion of climate change mitigation technologies (Dechezleprêtre et al. 2013). Other studies have found that the Kyoto Protocol's Clean Development Mechanism has boosted the transfer of climate change mitigation technologies from developed to developing countries (Dechezleprêtre et al. 2008 and Haščič and Johnstone 2011).

In recent years, the increase in climate change mitigation technology inventions has been substantial in Europe such that it now is considered as a global center for this kind of invention. The reason why innovation activity has become so relevant is due to the development and enforcement of climate change policies in many European countries. Taxes on polluting emissions, or tariffs for renewable energy have played a key role (UNEP-EPO 2015). Forcing to internalize environmental externalities is a way to mitigate the climate change effect and encourage the diffusion of environmentally friendly technologies. Kerr and Newell (2003) demonstrated this effect for the removal of lead from gasoline in the US while Snyder et al. (2003) and Popp et al. (2009) for the diffusion of membrane-cell technology in the chlorine manufacturing industry and NOX pollution control technologies at power plants, respectively.

Some analyses have focused on the policy-induced-innovation hypothesis as defined by Jaffe et al. (2005). Jaffe and Palmer (1997) and Brunnermeier and Cohen (2003) found a significant correlation between pollution abatement expenditures as a proxy for environmental regulatory stringency and innovative activity. More specifically, renewable energy policies have incentivized innovations in renewable energy technologies to generate electricity (Johnstone et al. 2010, 2012).

While the literature on EI has devoted some efforts to analyzing how innovation contributes to alleviating climate-related impacts, less intense remains the debate on the reverse relationship. Few studies examine how innovations have responded to climate change and weather variability as a means of adaptation strategy. A reason explaining this gap may be found in the inherent difficulty in testing the role of climate as a stimulant for technological innovation (Abler, et al. 2000). Popp and Miao (2014) exploited the theoretical framework and assessed to what extent the development of innovation responds to natural disasters. They stressed that "as climate change unfolds, there has been an increased recognition that climatic conditions may serve as a stimulus for technological innovation, particularly in the agricultural sector" (Popp and Miao 2014, p. 282). Along the same lines, Hongxiu (2017) estimated the response of technological innovations that reduce the impact of natural disasters. Using US patent data and damage data from floods, droughts, and earthquakes for the years 1977 to 2005, the author found that impact-reducing innovations at the state level respond to the damage of national disasters. Similarly, Hu et al. (2018) observed that in modern China past climate disasters induced an increase in the number of risk-mitigating technological innovations and that these stimulate spillover effect in technological progress.

As reported in Sect. 1.3, most of the literature is focused on mitigation-related innovation. However, as climate change manifests itself, whether and to what extent climate contingencies affect innovation is paramount to understanding the effectiveness of climate-adaptation strategies, especially in sectors such as agriculture (Rodima-Taylor et al. 2012). Thus, some insights suggest that climate-related innovations, measured by patent counts,[6] strongly respond to changes in climate (Su and Moaniba 2017) which induce adaptive capacity and foster the development and diffusion of innovation both in developed (Smithers and Blay-Palmer 2001) as well as developing countries (Chhetri and Easterling 2010). Conversely, from mitigation actions—that can be seen as the population's compliance response to the top-down burden imposed from governments' agreements and targets—adaptation entails bottom-up actions that actors either take proactively or reactively or not. Related measures can be developed either at relatively short notice in response to a perceived risk of extreme events or more gradually as a function of the experience of the changing variability in climatic parameters. In high-income countries such as Europe, adaptation tends to be proactive and focus on enhancing learning or research (Berrang-Ford et al. 2011). While some adaptation measures may be adaptive as such, others can be seen as an ongoing process in response to external forces and require private agents to engage in medium- to long-term efforts to anticipate climate-related damage. In the same vein, innovation allows dealing with the heterogeneous and uncertain impacts of climate and weather variability and can complement different forms of adaptation (Zilberman et al. 2018). As a

[6] The patent count is a convenient indicator of innovation for presenting the evolution of inventive capabilities over time. Patent counts can be considered a good proxy of invention success even if most of them are associated with inventions of little value (Hall 2011). Although patent numbers as a measure of innovative activity have been criticized (Griliches 1990), it is the most commonly used indicator when studying technological change and its effect on the environment (Popp 2005). The use of patents entails particular advantages because patent data are easily accessible via databases, are not subject to the problems of vague definition and allow comparability between firms and countries (Ernst 2001; Popp 2005).

result, many adaptation actions may differ not markedly, and in fact, coincide with, technological innovations (Smit and Skinner 2002; Ayers and Huq 2009; Patt et al. 2010; Berrang-Ford et al. 2011).

The relationship between climate variability and the knowledge generation process stands at the heart of adaptation-related innovations. The focus on climate change adaptation technologies emphasizes the role played by the incentives to innovate. As mentioned above, the development of these technologies is triggered by a diverse set of drivers with respect to climate change mitigation technologies. For instance, given the innovation inducement effect, policy implementation may result more effective in incentivizing mitigation technologies rather than adaptation ones (Popp 2002). On the other hand, climate variability or natural disaster hazard may be the main drivers of adaptation technologies. Climate variability increases the uncertainty of the surrounding environment in which firms operate, and therefore it may affect the firms' innovating behavior as an adaptation strategy to cope with such disruption, de facto affecting firms' performance. Thus, while the development of mitigation technologies, that affect the causes of climate change, is usually policy-driven and responds to compliance needs, the development of adaptation innovation emerges as a response to the need of coping with the impact of climate change and climate variability on productive activities (Popp and Miao 2014). Hence, adaptation innovation does not have an effect on the causes of climate change, but they increase adaptive capacity by providing the incentives for such endeavor. Moreover, compared to mitigation, adaptation entails a more local dimension. Accordingly, these inventions are able to lower the cost or overcome the disruptions brought about by climate change (i.e., adaptation-related innovation). This is particularly relevant as far as key resource-based sectors are concerned. Indeed, climate change will disproportionately affect countries as well as industries. The agricultural sector is (and will be) one of the most threatened.

Undoubtedly, technology is an important tool to boost the capacity of societies to cope with the negative effects of climate change (Miao 2017; GCA 2019). As regards adaptation-related innovations, it is worth noting that the data for the last few decades show that they have stagnated. With respect to the growth of climate change mitigation technologies whose share of total innovation (including non-climate-related technologies) has almost doubled, the share of inventions in adaptation has remained stable from 1995 to 2015 (Dechezleprêtre 2020). This is because, especially in the case of adaptation-related innovations that are based on a bottom-up process, international technology transfer becomes particularly relevant since a large fraction of this innovation activity is developed in high-income countries, while climate change adaptation technologies are mostly required in low- and middle-income countries, that are particularly exposed to climate shocks. In this view, it is paramount to distinguish the process of generating innovation from its application or adoption. As we pointed out in the previous Sect. (1.3), the innovation process involves various stages ranging from research activities, the development process to commercialization and use/adoption. Thus, it is worth distinguishing between the upstream phase where original technical knowledge, i.e., the novel and innovative contribution in terms of technical progress captured by the patent, is created, and the final adoption phase.

Particularly, regarding developing countries, several studies overlook the upstream phase, they focus on the adoption of already available technologies/practices (see among others, Di Falco et al. 2011; Läpple et al. 2013; Abdulai and Huffman 2014; Di Falco and Veronesi 2013; Teklewold et al. 2013, 2019; Kassie et al. 2015, 2018; Asfaw et al. 2018; Bozzola and Smale 2020). Indeed, the ability of farmers to adapt their production patterns to climate change is especially relevant when it is a matter of assessing the impact of climate change (Mendelsohn et al. 1994).

Only in the latest years has the possibility arisen to precisely distinguish patents produced for the invention of technologies aimed at climate change adaptation versus those designed to reduce pollution. From 2018, patent data from the PATSTAT database, collected by the EPO, allows us to disentangle patents relating to climate change adaptation technologies (Y02A) from all other patent types. This represents a good opportunity to develop a strand of literature analyzing adaptation-related innovations. For this reason, so far, only a few empirical works have been carried out on this topic. For example, Conway et al. (2015) focused on water-related innovations that become increasingly relevant as a result of climate change. Their analysis covering most of the technological adaptation options for water supply and demand shows a positive correlation between water scarcity and the filing of water patents. However, they also find that countries with low or moderate water scarcity, such as Switzerland or Norway, still seem to be significant markets for water efficiency technologies. This indicates that in addition to local demand, other factors such as regulation or cultural and social aspects also play a role.

In addition to the previous one, two recent analyses have investigated the relationship between climate-adaptation innovation and firm performance in the European agricultural sector. Using a Stochastic Frontier Approach, Auci et al. (2021a), employed a Ricardian framework to investigate the impact of firm-level climate-adaptation innovation on agricultural firms' technical efficiency. The authors' findings confirm the positive relationship between the innovation and climate variables in Europe and that innovation has a positive impact on firms' productivity. They also showed how agricultural firms located in Germany and Sweden are more efficient compared to those in southern countries. In a second analysis, Auci et al. (2021b), estimated a panel endogenous switching regression model to explore the development of climate-adaptation innovations and their effects on the economic performance of European firms in key resource-based sectors in Europe during the period 2007–2017. They concluded that the knowledge generation process at the heart of climate change adaptation technologies enhances firm performance, especially for firms in the aquaculture and fishing sub-sectors in northern European countries.

As reviewed earlier, the increased availability of micro-data offers new insights into an innovation driven by the need to respond to climate change. Firm/farmer level studies allow the identification of two subsamples, namely treated and untreated firms. Thus, it becomes possible to assess the impact of climate change by taking into account both innovations driven by mitigation and those triggered by adaptation.

References

Abdulai, A., & Huffman, W. (2014). The adoption and impact of soil and water conservation technology: an endogenous switching regression application. Land Economics, 90(1): 26–43.

Abler, D., Shortle, J., Rose, A., & Oladosu, G. (2000). Characterizing regional economic impacts and responses to climate change. Global and Planetary Change, 25(1–2): 67–81.

Acemoglu, D. (2002). Directed technical change. Review of Economic Studies, 69: 781–810.

Acemoglu, D., Aghion, P., Bursztyn L., & Hemous D. (2012). The environment and directed technical change. The American Economic Review, 102(1): 131–166.

Åhman, M., Skjærseth, J. B., & Eikeland, P. O. (2018). Demonstrating climate mitigation technologies: an early assessment of the NER 300 programme. Energy Policy, 117: 100–107.

Ahmed, T., Zounemat-Kermani, M., & Scholz, M. (2020). Climate change, water quality and water-related challenges: a review with focus on Pakistan. International Journal of Environmental Research and Public Health, 17(22): 8518.

Aldieri, L., Carlucci, F., Vinci, C. P., & Yigitcanlar, T. (2019). Environmental innovation, knowledge spillovers and policy implications: a systematic review of the economic effects literature. Journal of Cleaner Production, 239: 118051.

Ambec, S., Cohen, M., Elgie, S., & Lanoie, P. (2013). The porter hypothesis at 20: can environmental regulation enhance innovation and competitiveness? Review of Environmental Economics and Policy, 7(1): 2–22.

Arbolino, R., Boffardi, R., Lanuzza, F., & Ioppolo, G., (2018). Monitoring and evaluation of regional industrial sustainability: evidence from Italian regions. Land Use Policy, 75: 420–428.

Asfaw, S., Pallante, G., & Palma, A. (2018). Diversification strategies and adaptation deficit: evidence from rural communities in Niger. World Development, 101: 219–234.

Auci, S., Barbieri, N., Coromaldi, M., & Michetti, M. (2021b). Climate variability, innovation and firm performance: evidence from the European agricultural sector. European Review of Agricultural Economics, 48(5): 1074–1108.

Auci, S., Barbieri, N., Coromaldi, M., & Vignani, D. (2021a). Innovation for climate change adaptation and technical efficiency: an empirical analysis in the European agricultural sector. Economia Politica, 38(2): 597–623.

Ayers, J. M., & Huq, S. (2009). Supporting adaptation to climate change. The role for official development assistance? Development Policy Review, 27: 675–692.

Barbieri, N. (2015). Investigating the impacts of technological position and European environmental regulation on green automotive patent activity. Ecological Economics, 117: 140–152.

Barbieri, N., Ghisetti, C., Gilli, M., Marin, G., & Nicolli, F. (2016). A survey of the literature on environmental innovation based on main path analysis. Journal of Economic Surveys, 30(3): 596–623.

Berrang-Ford, L., Frd, J.D., & Paterson, J. (2011). Are we adapting to climate change? Global Environmental Change, 21(1): 25–33.

Berrang-Ford, L., Frd, J. D., & Paterson, J. (2011). Are we adapting to climate change? Global Environmental Change, 21(1): 25–33.

Bozzola, M., & Smale, M. (2020) The welfare effects of crop biodiversity as an adaptation to climate shocks in Kenya. World Development, 135: 105065.

Brunnermeier, S., & Cohen, M. (2003). Determinants of environmental innovation in US manufacturing industries. Journal of Environmental Economics and Management, 45 (2): 278–293.

Caminade, C., Kovats, S., Rocklov, J., Tompkins, A. M., Morse, A. P., Colón-González, F. J., Stenlund H., Martens P., & Lloyd, S. J. (2014). Impact of climate change on global malaria distribution. Proceedings of the National Academy of Sciences, 111(9): 3286–3291.

Chhetri N. B., & Easterling, W. E. (2010). Adapting to climate change: retrospective analysis of climate technology interaction in the rice-based farming system of Nepal. Annals of the Association of American Geographers, 100(5): 1156–1176.

Conway, D., Dechezleprêtre, A., Haščič, I., & Johnstone. N. (2015). "Invention and Diffusion of Water Supply and Water Efficiency Technologies: Insights from a Global Patent Dataset." Water Economics and Policy 1 (4): 1–34. https://doi.org/10.1142/S2382624X15500101

Costantini, V., Mazzanti, M., & Montini, A. (2013). Environmental performance, innovation and spillovers. Evidence from a regional NAMEA. Ecological Economics, 89: 101–114.

Dasgupta, P. (2021). The economics of biodiversity: the Dasgupta review. HM Treasury.

Dechezlepretre, A., Fankhauser, S., Glachant, M., Stoever, J., & Touboul, S. (2020). Invention and global diffusion of technologies for climate change adaptation. World Bank, Washington, DC.

Dechezleprêtre, A., Glachant, M., Haščič, I., Johnstone, N., & Ménière, Y. (2011). Invention and transfer of climate change mitigation technologies: a global analysis. Review of Environmental Economics and Policy, 5(1): 109–130.

Dechezleprêtre, A., Glachant, M., & Ménière, Y. (2008). The clean development mechanism and the international diffusion of technologies: an empirical study. Energy Policy, 36(4): 1273–1283.

Dechezleprêtre, A., Glachant, M., & Ménière, Y. (2013). What drives the international transfer of climate change mitigation technologies? empirical evidence from patent data. Environmental & Resource Economics, 54(2): 161–178.

Di Falco, S., & Veronesi, M. (2013). How can African agriculture adapt to climate change? a counterfactual analysis from Ethiopia. Land Economics, 89: 743–766.

Di Falco, S., Veronesi, M., & Yesuf, M. (2011). Does adaptation to climate change provide food security? a micro-perspective from Ethiopia. American Journal of Agricultural Economics, 93: 829–846.

Dopfer, K. (2012). The origins of meso economics. Journal of Evolutionary Economics, 22(1): 133–160.

Dosi, G. (1988). The nature of the innovative process. Technical change and economic theory. Pinter Publisher.
EEA, European Environmental Agency. (2019). Climate Change Adaptation in the Agriculture Sector in Europe. EEA Report N4–2019. Luxembourg: Publications Office of the European Union. ISSN 1977–8449.
EPO-UNEP-ICTSD. (2010). Patents and clean energy technologies: bridging the gap between energy and policy. Munich: Mediengruppe Universal.
Ernst, H. (2001). Patent applications and subsequent changes of performance: evidence from time-series cross-section analyses on the firm level. *Research Policy*, 30(1): 143–157.
GCA (Global Commission on Adaptation). (2019). Adapt Now: A Global Call for Leadership on Climate Resilience. Report, GCA, Rotterdam; World Resources Institute, Washington, DC.
Ghisetti, C., & Pontoni, F. (2015). Investigating policy and R&D effects on environmental innovation: a meta-analysis. Ecological Economics, 118: 57–66.
Ghisetti, C., & Quatraro, F. (2013). Beyond inducement in climate change: does environmental performance spur environmental technologies? a regional analysis of cross-sectoral differences. Ecological Economics, 96: 99–113.
Griliches, Z. (1990). Patent statistics as economic indicators: a survey. *Journal of Economic* Literature, 28(4): 1661–1707.
Hall, B. H. (2011). Innovation and productivity, NBER Working Paper 17178, Cambridge, MA: National Bureau of Economic Research.
Haščič, I., & Johnstone, N. (2011). CDM and international technology transfer: empirical evidence on wind power. Climate Policy, 11(6): 1303–1314.
Hernández-Delgado, E. A. (2015). The emerging threat of climate change on tropical coastal ecosystem services, public health, local economies and livelihood sustainability of small islands: cumulative impacts and synergies. Marine Pollution Bulletin, 101(2015): 5 –28.
Hicks, J. R. (1932). The theory of wages. London: Macmillan.
Hoegh-Guldberg, O., Pendleton, L., & Kaup, A. (2019). People and the changing nature of coral reefs. Regional Studies in Marine Science, 30, 100699.
Hongxiu, Li. (2017). "Innovation as Adaptation to Natural Disasters." Working Paper No. 1709, Department of Economics, University of Waterloo, Ontario.
Horbach, J. (2008). Determinants of environmental innovation—new evidence from German panel data sources. Research Policy, 37(1): 163–173.
Horbach, J., Rammer, C., & Rennings, K. (2012). Determinants of eco-innovations by type of environmental impact—the role of regulatory push/pull, technology push and market pull. Ecological Economics, 78: 112–122.

Hu, H., Lei, T., Hu, J., Zhang, S., & Kavan. P. (2018). "Disaster-Mitigating and General Innovative Responses to Climate Disasters: Evidence from Modern and Historical China." International Journal of Disaster Risk Reduction 28: 664–73. https://doi.org/10.1016/j.

IPCC. (2007). Contribution of Working Group II to the Fourth Assessment Report of the Intergovernmental Panel on Climate Change, 2007 (M.L. Parry, O.F. Canziani, J.P. Palutikof, P.J. van der Linden and C.E. Hanson, Eds). Cambridge University Press, Cambridge, United Kingdom and New York, NY, USA.

IPCC. (2014a). Climate change 2014a: synthesis report. Contribution of Working Groups I, II and III to the Fifth Assessment Report of the Intergovernmental Panel on Climate Change (Core Writing Team, R.K. Pachauri and L.A. Meyer, Eds.) p. 155. IPCC, Geneva, Switzerland.

IPCC. (2014b). "Climate change 2014b: impacts, adaptation, and vulnerability." Contribution of WGI to the 5th Assessment Report of the IPCC, Geneva.

IPCC. (2018a). Global Warming of 1.5°C. An IPCC Special Report on the Impacts of Global Warming of 1.5°C Above Pre-Industrial Levels and Related Global Greenhouse Gas Emission Pathways, in the Context of Strengthening the Global Response to the Threat of Climate Change, Sustainable Development, and Efforts to Eradicate Poverty. (V. Masson-Delmotte, P. Zhai, H. O. Pörtner, D. Roberts, J. Skea, P. R. Shukla, A. Pirani, W. Moufouma-Okia, C. Péan, R. Pidcock, S. Connors, J. B. R. Matthews, Y. Chen, X. Zhou, M. I. Gomis, E. Lonnoy, T. Maycock, M. Tignor, & T. Waterfield, Eds.). Cambridge: Cambridge University Press.

IPCC. (2018b). Annex I: Glossary [Matthews, J.B.R. (ed.)]. In: Global Warming of 1.5°C. An IPCC Special Report on the impacts of global warming of 1.5°C above pre-industrial levels and related global greenhouse gas emission pathways, in the context of strengthening the global response to the threat of climate change, sustainable development, and efforts to eradicate poverty [Masson-Delmotte, V., P. Zhai, H.-O. Pörtner, D. Roberts, J. Skea, P.R. Shukla, A. Pirani, W. Moufouma-Okia, C. Péan, R. Pidcock, S. Connors, J.B.R. Matthews, Y. Chen, X. Zhou, M.I. Gomis, E. Lonnoy, T. Maycock, M. Tignor, and T. Waterfield (eds.)]. In Press.

Jacob, D. J., & Winner, D. A. (2009). Effect of climate change on air quality. Atmospheric environment, 43(1): 51–63.

Jactel, H., J. Koricheva, and B. Castagneyrol (2019), Responses of forest insect pests to climate change: not so simple, current opinion in insect science, 35: 103–108.

Jaffe, A. B., & Palmer, K. (1997). Environmental regulation and innovation: a panel data study. Review of Economics and Statistics, 79(4): 610–619.

Jaffe, A. B., Newell, R. G., & Stavins, R. N. (2002). Environmental policy and technological change. Environmental and Resource Economics, 22(1–2): 41–70.

Jaffe, A. B., Newell, R. G., & Stavins, R. N. (2005). A tale of two market failures: technology and environmental policy. Ecological Economics, 54(2–3): 164–174.

Johnstone, N., Haščič, I., Poirier, J., Hemar, M., & Michel, C. (2012). Environmental policy stringency and technological innovation: evidence from survey data and patent counts. Applied Economics, 44(17): 2157–2170.

Johnstone, N., Haščič, I., & Popp, P. (2010). Renewable energy policies and technological innovation: evidence based on patent counts, environmental & resource economics. European Association of Environmental and Resource Economists, 45(1): 133–155.

Kassie, M., Marenya, P., Tessema, Y., Jaleta, M., Zeng, D., Erenstein, O., & Rahut, D. (2018). Measuring farm and market level economic impacts of improved maize production technologies in Ethiopia: evidence from panel data. Journal of Agricultural Economics, 69(1): 76–95.

Kassie, M., Teklewold, H., Marenya, P., Jaleta, M., & Erenstein, O. (2015). Production risks and food security under alternative technology choices in Malawi: application of a multinomial endogenous switching regression. Journal of Agricultural Economics, 66: 640–659.

Kerr, S., & Newell, R. (2003). Policy-induced technology adoption: evidence from the U.S. lead phasedown. Journal of Industrial Economics, 51(3): 317–343.

Kinney, P. L. (2008). Climate change, air quality, and human health. American journal of preventive medicine, 35(5): 459–467.

Klein, R. J. T., Huq, S., Denton, F., Downing, T.E., Richels, R.G., Robinson, J.B., Toth, F.L. (2007). Inter-relationships between adaptation and mitigation. Climate change 2007: impacts, adaptation and vulnerability. Contribution of Working Group II to the Fourth Assessment Report of the Intergovernmental Panel on Climate Change (M.L. Parry, O.F. Canziani, J.P. Palutikof, P.J. van der Linden and C.E. Hanson, Eds.). Cambridge University Press, Cambridge, UK, 745–777.

Kline, S. J., & Rosenberg, N. (2010). An overview of innovation. Studies on science and the innovation process: selected works of Nathan Rosenberg, 173–203.

Läpple, D., Hennessy, T., & Newman, C. (2013). Quantifying the economic return to participatory extension programmes in Ireland: an endogenous switching regression analysis. Journal of Agricultural Economics, 64: 467–482.

Lemay, M. A., Henry, P., Lamb, C. T., Robson, K. M., & Russello, M. A. (2013). Novel genomic resources for a climate change sensitive mammal:

characterization of the American Pika Transcriptome, BMC Genomics, 14(1): 311.

Lovejoy, T. E., & Hannah, L. (2019). Biodiversity and climate change: transforming the biosphere. New Haven, CT: Yale University Press.

Mazzanti, M., & Zoboli, R. (2009). Environmental efficiency and labour productivity: trade-off or joint dynamics? a theoretical investigation and empirical evidence from Italy using NAMEA. Ecological Economics, 68(4): 1182–1194.

Mendelsohn, R., Nordhaus, W. D., & Shaw, D. (1994). The impact of global warming on agriculture: a Ricardian analysis. The American economic review, 753–771.

Miao, Q. (2017). Technological innovation, social learning and natural hazard mitigation: evidence on earthquake fatalities. Environment and Development Economics, 22(3): 249–273.

Miao, Q., & Popp, D. (2014). Necessity as the mother of invention: innovative responses to natural disasters. Journal of Environmental Economics and Management, 68(2): 280–295.

Nelson, G. C., Rosegrant, M. W., Koo, J., Robertson, R., Sulser, T., Zhu, T., ... & Lee, D. (2009). Climate change: impact on agriculture and costs of adaptation (Vol. 21). Intl Food Policy Res Inst.

Newell, R. G., Jaffe, A. B., & Stavins, R. N. (1999). The induced innovation hypothesis and energy-saving technological change. The Quarterly Journal of Economics, 114(3): 941–975.

Nordhaus, W. (2019). Climate change: the ultimate challenge for economics. American Economic Review, 109(6): 1991–2014.

Palmer, K., Oaetes, W. E., Portney, P. R. (1995). Tightening environmental standards: the benefit-cost or the no-cost paradigm? Journal of Economical Perspectives, 9(4): 119–132.

Patt, A. G., van Vuuren, D. P., Berkhout, F., Aaheim, A., Hof, A. F., Isaac, M., & Mechler, R. (2010). Adaptation in integrated assessment modeling: where do we stand? Climatic Change, 99(3): 383–402.

Popp, D. (2002). Induced innovation and energy prices. American economic review, 92(1): 160–180.

Popp, D. (2005). Lessons from patents: using patents to measure technological change in environmental models. Ecological Economics, 54(2): 209–226.

Popp, D. (2019). Environmental policy and innovation: a decade of research. National Bureau of Economic Research Working Paper Series (w25631).

Popp, D., Fleishman, R., Alexander, R., & Bretschneider, S. (2009). Does regulation stimulate technical productive efficiency? the effect of air quality policies on the efficiency of U.S. power plants. Energy Policy, 37(11): 4574–4582.

Popp, D., Newell, R. G., & Jaffe, A. B. (2010). Energy, the environment, and technological change. In Handbook of the Economics of Innovation (Vol. 2, pp. 873–937). North-Holland.

Porter, M. E., & van der Linde, C. (1995). Toward a new conception of the environment-competitiveness relationship. Journal of Economic Perspectives, 97–118.

Porter, M. E. (1991). America's green strategy. Scientific American, 264(4).

Ray, D. K., West, P. C., Clark, M., Gerber, J. S., Prishchepov, A. V., & Chatterjee, S. (2019). Climate change has likely already affected global food production. PloS one, 14(5): e0217148.

Rennings, K. (2000). Redefining innovation—eco-innovation research and the contribution from ecological economics. Ecological Economics, 32(2): 319–332.

Rodima-Taylor, D., Olwig, M. F. & Chhetri, N. (2012). Adaptation as innovation, innovation as adaptation: an institutional approach to climate change. Applied Geography 33(0): 107–111.

Smit B., & Skinner M. W. (2002). Adaptation options in agriculture to climate change: a typology. Mitigation and Adaptation Strategies for Global Change, 7: 85–114.

Smith, J. B., Schellnhuber, H. -J., Mirza, M., Fankhauser, S., Leemans, R., Lin Erda, Ogallo, L., Pittock, B., Richels, R., Rosenzweig, C., Safriel, U., Tol, R. S. J., Weyant, J., & Yohe, G. (2001). Vulnerability to climate change and reasons for concern: a synthesis. Climate change 2001: impacts, adaptation, and vulnerability. Contribution of Working Group II to the Third Assessment Report of the Intergovernmental Panel on Climate Change (J.J. McCarthy, O.F. Canziani, N.A. Leary, D.J. Dokken and K.S. White, Eds.). Cambridge University Press, Cambridge, 914–967.

Smith, P., & Gregory, P. J. (2013). Climate change and sustainable food production. Proceedings of the Nutrition Society, 72(1): 21–28.

Smithers J., & Blay-Palmer A. (2001). Technology innovation as a strategy for climate adaptation in agriculture. Applied Geography, 21(2): 175–197.

Snyder, L. D., Miller, N. H., & Stavins, R. N. (2003). The effects of environmental regulation on technology diffusion: the case of chlorine manufacturing. American Economic Review, 93(2): 431–435.

Sork, V. L., Fitz-Gibbon, S. T., Puiu, D., Crepeau, M., Gugger, P. F., Sherman, R., Stevens, K., Langley, C. H., Pellegrini, M., & Salzberg, S. L. (2016). First draft assembly and annotation of the genome of a California Endemic Oak Quercus lobata née (Fagaceae). G3: Genes, Genomes, Genetics, 6(11): 3485–3495.

Stevanovic M., Popp A., Lotze-Campen H., Dietrich, J. P., Muller, C., Bonsch, M., et al. (2016). The impact of highend climate change on agricultural welfare. Science Advances, 2: e1501452–e1501452.

Su, H. N., & Moaniba, I. M. (2017). Does innovation respond to climate change? empirical evidence from patents and greenhouse gas emissions. Technological Forecasting and Social Change, 122: 49–62.

Teklewold, H., Kassie, M., Shiferaw, B., & K¨ohlin, G. (2013). Cropping system diversification, conservation tillage and modern seed adoption in Ethiopia: impacts on household income, agrochemical use and demand for labor. Ecological Economics, 93: 85–95.

Teklewold, H., Mekonnen, A., & Kohlin, G. (2019). Climate change adaptation: a study of multiple climate-smart practices in the Nile Basin of Ethiopia. Climate and Development, 11(2): 180–192.

UNEP-EPO. (2015). Climate change mitigation technologies in Europe-Evidence from patent and economic data. Munich: Graphic Design Munich.

Vanschoenwinkela J., Mendelsohn, R., & Van Passel, S. (2016). Do Western and Eastern Europe have the same agricultural climate response? taking adaptive capacity into account. Global Environmental Change, 41(2016): 74–87 C.

World Health Organization. Drinking Water. Fact Sheet. (2016). Available online: http://www.who.int/mediacentre/factsheets/fs391/en/ (accessed on 20 January 2021).

Zilberman D., Lipper L., McCarthy N., & Gordon B. (2018). Innovation in Response to Climate Change. Climate Smart Agriculture (L. Lipper, N. McCarthy, D. Zilberman, S. Asfaw, G. Branca, Eds.). Natural Resource Management and Policy, vol 52. Springer, Cham.

CHAPTER 2

Agricultural and Biotechnology Patents as an Adaptation Strategy to Climate Change: A Regional Analysis of European Farmer's Efficiency

Sabrina Auci and Manuela Coromaldi

Abstract This chapter analyses the effect of innovation encouraged by climate change challenges on European farmers' technical efficiency. Using the stochastic frontier approach, we estimate the impact of agricultural patents on farmers' technical efficiency by taking into account both unobservable heterogeneity and heteroscedasticity in the inefficiency term. Our findings suggest that European farmers remain quite far from the maximum frontier and irrespective of the country in which they

S. Auci (✉)
Department of Political Science and International Relations, University of Palermo, Palermo, Italy
e-mail: sabrina.auci@unipa.it

M. Coromaldi
Department of Economics, University of Rome Niccolò Cusano, Rome, Italy
e-mail: manuela.coromaldi@unicusano.it

M. Coromaldi and S. Auci (eds.), *Climate-Induced Innovation*,
https://doi.org/10.1007/978-3-031-01330-0_2

reside; farmers who innovate are more efficient than those who do not. Thus, the inefficiency of agricultural agents in the European context leaves space for policies that incentivise firms to adopt climate change adaptation strategies through technological innovation.

Keywords Climate change · Agriculture · Adaptation · Patent · Stochastic frontier approach

2.1 Introduction

The need to increase the global food supply under decreasing soil and water availability and the growing threats of climate change represent two of the most significant challenges agriculture has to face in the immediate future. The global phenomenon of climate change, as in other parts of the world, is hard testing European agriculture that is subject to significant risks generated by new local weather conditions. Climate change effects show marked local consequences that manifest themselves in heterogeneous ways across regions and sectors (IPCC, 2014). As for agriculture, for example, production and productivity in Northern Europe might increase due to a lengthening of the growing season and to an extension of the frost-free period. Conversely, southern European countries will likely observe a productivity reduction (EEA, 2019), induced by extreme temperature and by lower precipitation and water availability, which will intensify problems of droughts, especially in the Mediterranean region (Goubanova and Li, 2007; Rodriguez Diaz et al., 2007; IPCC 2014). Similarly, higher temperatures and drought risk will likely reduce the livestock productivity negatively affecting grassland production, animal health, and varying the distribution of pathogens vectors across space, with effects that may pose challenges especially in northern Europe (EEA, 2019). As a result, the impacts of climate change and variability on economic and social systems will be space-varying with effects that translate into different responses as a function of socio-economic heterogeneity (ECONADPT, 2016; Zilberman et al., 2018) and dissimilar adaptive capacity (Vanschoenwinkela et al., 2017). In view of this, analyses at the regional level are better suited to capture heterogeneous effects between different areas.

In addition to climate change, exponential population growth is also a stress factor for agriculture, which has to provide an ever-increasing quantity of food with ever-higher quality standards. In Europe, the supply of food is not the main concern, but rather the demand for food that can meet an ever-increasing demand for healthy, nutrient-dense food produced in a sustainable way with minimal environmental impact. The need for agricultural production to be increasingly sustainable and less impactful on the environment represents an aim that requires high-intensive knowledge and innovative capacities.

To cope with these kinds of challenges, one strategy could be to react by innovating. Developing and adopting innovation in climate-sensitive sectors is not merely a matter of facing the threats of weather and climate variability. The deployment of technologies and the extent to which they affect economic performances are highly idiosyncratic and could confront Europe with both opportunities and challenges, and only eventually bring about economic opportunities (e.g., EEA, 2019). In light of that, it is crucial to understand the drivers that enhance innovative capabilities and their impact on farm outcomes.

Developing crop varieties that are more resilient to climate change can reduce the vulnerability of agricultural production. Innovation in technologies that promote mitigation and adaptation will decrease the costs of policy measures and provide new opportunities for the private sector. Using agricultural crop biotechnology as a case study of innovative activity, this chapter analyses the impact of crop biotechnology patents on European farmers' efficiency at the regional level.

In analysing whether and to what extent innovation affects firms' performance, we estimate the technical efficiency of a representative average farm by considering simultaneously a farmer's optimal production function and a technical in/efficiency equation. Following Greene (2005), we disentangle time-invariant heterogeneity from time-varying inefficiency ("true" fixed-and random-effects) and we control for heteroscedasticity by specifying explanatory variables for the inefficiency variance function (Hadri et al., 2003). Data on Spain, Italy, and France are drawn from the Farm Accountancy Data Network (FADN) at the regional level.

This dataset is a European system of sample surveys, carried out every year from 2004, to collect structural and accountancy data of farms in order to monitor the income and business activities of agricultural holdings. Data are related to the balance sheets of an average representative farm commonly used in sector models based on linear programming (Jonasson and Apland, 1997 and De Maietta et al., 2019). Until now, FADN is the only source of harmonised micro-economic data based on bookkeeping principles, the same in all Member States.

To capture the effects of innovation in agricultural biotechnology, patents are considered a useful indicator as they illustrate the evolution of inventive activity in adaptation-related biotechnology over time, the countries where innovation takes place, where patent applications are submitted and the institutions involved (Agrawala et al., 2012). However, even if not all successful research and innovative efforts are protected through patents, Arundel and Kabla (1998) found that patent propensity rates among European firms increase with firm size and Groombridge (1992) found that patents are widely used to secure companies' investments in agricultural biotechnology. Data on patents are based on the European Patent Office (EPO) dataset. Specifically designed for the statistical analysis, the database gathers patents registered in more than 80 national and international patent authorities in a standardised form, which allows for a global cross-country analysis of innovative activity and trends.

In this chapter, we first describe the databases used and the empirical strategy adopted and then we discuss the results. Finally, some main conclusions are drawn.

2.2 Data Description

Focusing on the three major agricultural producers among the European countries, we collect an unbalanced panel dataset of Spain, France, and Italy at the regional (Nuts3) level. Specifically, the analysis is based on two main sources of data, collected yearly from 2004 to 2012: the Farm Accountancy Data Network (FADN) and Eurostat database on patents.

The Farm Accountancy Data Network (FADN)

Established to evaluate the impact of the common agricultural policy, FADN is a European system of national surveys, carried out each year from 2004, which collects structural and accountancy data. It is the only source of harmonised micro-economic data relating to farms' income and business activities to monitor the production diversity and income of European agricultural holdings. FADN provides representative data according to three categories: region, economic size, and type of farming.

Data refer to the balance sheets of an average representative farm at the regional level. This type of farm is commonly used in sector models based on linear programming (Jonasson and Apland, 1997 and Maietta et al., 2019).

As outcome variable, we select the total output of crops and crop products, livestock and livestock products, and other output. The total output also includes sales and use of (crop and livestock) products and livestock, the change in stocks of products (crop and livestock), the change in valuation of livestock and various non-exceptional products. Finally, the purchases of livestock are subtracted from the total amount.

In the estimated production function, there are several production inputs collected: capital, materials, labour, and farm size. As capital input, we select total assets in ownership which include fixed and current assets whose value is based on the closing valuation. Materials represented by total intermediate consumption comprise specific costs (including inputs produced on the holding) and operating costs arising from production in the accounting year. To capture the farm size, we introduce the total standard gross margin variable. All these three variables are expressed in euro and are deflated by using both the two 2010-based indices of producer prices of agricultural products and purchase prices of the means of agricultural production from Eurostat.

As regards labour employed within a farm, we may distinguish between unpaid and paid labour. The total unpaid labour input refers to family labour expressed in the family annual work unit (FAWU), while the total paid labour variable considers employees remunerated in cash or in-kind expressed in the Annual work unit (AWU).

In Table 2.1, the mean values of the production function variables are reported for the complete sample and Spain, France, and Italy. From this comparison, we may underline that the French farm size is in mean bigger than the representative farms in the other countries. They employ more labour both paid and unpaid and have higher total intermediate consumption. However, in terms of total assets French and Italian farms have the same value of capital. These differences imply that the mean value of French farms' total output is more than double of the farms located in Spain and Italy.

Eurostat Database on Patent

Patents as a convenient indicator of innovation activity allow showing the evolution of inventive capabilities in adaptation-related agriculture and food technology over time. They provide information on the regions in which the inventive activities take place and where patent applications are submitted (Agrawala et al., 2012). In addition, they offer a clear comparison mean among regions and sectors (Su and Moaniba, 2017), even if the patent indicator is not exempt from criticism. As Griliches and Pakes (1980) underline, patents are a good proxy for inventions due to their vicinity to the knowledge generation process such as R&D. Janger et al. (2017) and Dechezlepretre et al. (2011) stress some drawbacks in using patent as innovation indicator. They argue that some innovations are patented only for impeding competitors' innovations, not all patents are brought into use, and finally not all innovations outputs are patented because some firms prefer the business secret (Popp, 2005). For all these reasons, the patent indicator used in this analysis is not representative of innovation outputs but farm knowledge in line with the knowledge-based view (Nelson, 1991).

Data concerning patent applications come from Eurostat which provides patent applications to the European Patent Office (EPO) by priority year by Nuts3 regions. Patents are classified according to the International Patent Classification (IPC). To capture the effects of innovative activity in agriculture, we select two different typologies of patents. First, the agricultural patents are collected by drawing the total number and per millions of inhabitants of patents classified in the IPC A01 code entitled "Agriculture; Forestry; Animal Husbandry; Hunting; Trapping; Fishing".

Focusing on innovation for adaptation, agricultural crop biotechnology patents are the most important ones. Indeed, the agricultural sector should innovate in plant breeding to develop new crop varieties that are more resilient to climate change impacts. Eurostat releases the total number and per millions of inhabitants of biotechnology patent applications to the EPO by priority year by Nuts3 regions. From Table 2.1, it is worth noting that French regions are in the mean more innovative than the Spanish and Italian regions.

Table 2.1 Descriptive statistics (mean values)

VAR	*DEFINITION*	*Overall*	*Spain*	*France*	*Italy*
Production function (FADN dataset)					
Output	The value of total output sold and used (crops and livestock products and their change in stocks) (euro)	1075.12	539.83	1629.69	526.26
Capital	The value of total assets (fixed and current) in ownership (euro)	3753.36	2813.27	3967.90	3763.21
Materials	The value of total intermediate consumption (inputs purchased and produced on the holding and overheads arising from production) (euro)	626.55	300.25	1008.93	231.58
Unpaid Labour	The total unpaid labour input (family labour) (Family work unit (FWU))	1.29	1.18	1.48	1.07
Paid Labour	The total paid labour input remunerated in cash or in-kind (Annual work unit (AWU))	0.42	0.30	0.58	0.26
Farm size	The value of total gross margin (euro)	1232.83	703.07	1766.23	676.73
Inefficiency function (EUROSTAT dataset)					
Agricultural patent	Two-year lagged variable of number of patent applications in IPC code A01 "Agriculture; forestry; animal husbandry; hunting; trapping; fishing"	4.81	2.39	5.81	4.38

(continued)

Table 2.1 (continued)

VAR	*DEFINITION*	*Overall*	*Spain*	*France*	*Italy*
Agricultural patent per inhabitant	Two-year lagged variable of number of patent applications per millions of inhabitants in IPC code A01 "Agriculture; forestry; animal husbandry; hunting; trapping; fishing"	1.67	0.95	2.24	1.62
Biotechnology patent	Two-year lagged variable of number of biotechnology patent applications	15.03	7.33	20.81	8.86
Biotechnology patent per inhabitant	Two-year lagged variable of Number per millions of inhabitants of biotechnology patent applications	3.67	2.31	4.80	2.41
Observations		480	213	285	263

2.3 Empirical Strategy and Model Specification

Empirical Strategy

To empirically estimate the relationship between regional technical efficiency and innovation capacity we apply the stochastic frontier approach (SFA) originally developed by Aigner et al. (1977) and Meeusen and van den Broeck (1977). Initially, this technique was developed to investigate firms' efficiency but later was used to measure technical efficiency at a more aggregate level such as the country level (Moroney and Lovell, 1997; Méon and Weill, 2005 and 2010; Méon, Schneider and Weill, 2011; Brock and Ogloblin, 2014). This methodology is considered as the best strategy to estimate macroeconomic productivity for the following reasons. First, it allows including several input dimensions in evaluating productivity. The output is compared to all inputs like labour, physical and human capital jointly considered, providing a synthetic measure of productivity. Second, this methodology provides a relative productivity measure and therefore each region can be compared to the best practice region. This implies estimating the distance of each region's actual frontier to its optimal production given the same bundle of inputs. Finally, SFA allows disentangling the distance from the production frontier into an inefficiency term and a random error. Thus, in these models, the composite error term is given by the difference between symmetric idiosyncratic error and one-sided disturbance representing technical inefficiency. Recently, the availability of a richer set of information in panel data and the development of more sophisticated models allow one to estimate technical efficiency by controlling for time-invariant inefficiency, time-varying inefficiency, and unobserved heterogeneity. Thus, we may distinguish between time-invariant inefficiency models and time-varying inefficiency models. Among the first type of models, we may recall the Pitt and Lee (1981) model, while among the time-varying inefficiency models, the true random-effects model developed by Greene (2005) is considered where unmeasured heterogeneity and time-varying firm inefficiency are both included.

Pitt and Lee (1981) were the first to extend the stochastic frontier approach to longitudinal data. They assume that the inefficiency term is region-specific so that technical efficiency is constant over time. The production function can be expressed as:

$$Y_{it} = a + bx_{it} + (v_{it} - u_i) \;\forall i = 1, \ldots, N \text{ and } t = 1, \ldots, T \tag{2.1}$$

where $v_{it} \sim N(0, \sigma_v^2)$ and u_i is distributed as a half-normal random variable. $N^+(0, \sigma_u^2)$.

However, a time-invariant inefficiency term could be perceived as a restriction, especially in the presence of empirical applications based on long-panel datasets. After several attempts to introduce a time-varying inefficiency term[1], Greene (2005) proposed the True Random Effect (TRE) model as an extension of the parametric stochastic frontier approach for panel data. This specification compared to other time-varying inefficiency models has the advantage of disentangling time-varying inefficiency from unit-specific time-invariant unobserved heterogeneity in order to avoid a misspecification bias in the presence of time-invariant unobservable factors. The production function can be expressed as:

$$Y_{it} = a_i + bx_{it} + (v_{it} - u_{it}) \;\forall i = 1, \ldots, N \text{ and } t = 1, \ldots, T \tag{2.2}$$

[1] See Belotti et al., 2013 for a literature review.

where $v_{it} \sim N(0, \sigma_v^2)$ is distributed as a normal random variable and u_{it} is distributed as a half-normal random variable $N^+(0, \sigma_u^2)$. a_i is the region-specific random effect, distributed as $N(0, \sigma_a^2)$. Further development of these models was the possibility to include exogenous variables which usually are neither the inputs nor the outputs of the production process but are supposed to affect the productive unit performance.

Following Greene (2008) and Hadri et al. (2003), the extension considered has the aim of analysing the inefficiency determinants related to observed heterogeneity of European regional farms. We include efficiency determinants that directly affect the inefficiency u_{it} in the variance of the inefficiency error:

$$\sigma_{u_{it}}^2 = exp(\gamma' z_{it}) \tag{2.3}$$

where z_{it} is a px1 vector of variables that may have an indirect effect on the production function of a European farmer; γ is a 1xp vector of parameters to be estimated.

As a robustness check, we show results for the three models, Pitt and Lee (1981) model, TRE without and with the determinants of the inefficiency model.

Model Specification

The empirical analysis in a Ricardian setting requires the specification of a production function. The Cobb–Douglas (C-D) and translog functions are commonly used in the stochastic frontier literature as underlined by Greene (2008). Among the two specifications, we opted for the C-D production function, which has universally smooth and convex isoquants and requires a limited number of variables. This has a practical advantage in statistical estimations over more complicated models like the one we estimated[2].

[2] The translog functional form is more flexible because it allows the output elasticities and returns to scale to vary with the input levels, and it also places no restrictions on substitution elasticities. However, it requires the estimation of many parameters, which provides the potential risk of multicollinearity.

Following the standard C-D production function for European farms, output and inputs expressed in natural log values can be written as:

$$lnY_{it} = \beta_0 + \beta_1 lnK_{it} + \beta_2 lnM_{it} + \beta_3 lnUL_{it} + \beta_4 lnPL_{it} + \beta_5 lnsize_{it} + v_{it} - u_{it} + \alpha_i \tag{2.4}$$

where the dependent variable, Y_{it}, is the value of the total output of the *i-th* region at time t ($i = 1,\ldots,N$; $t = 1,\ldots,T$), and the independent variables are K_{it} that is the value of total assets, M_{it} is the value of total intermediate consumption, UL_{it} is the total unpaid labour input or family labour, PL_{it} is the total paid labour input and $size_{it}$ is the value of total gross margin.

As mentioned in Belotti et al. (2013), neglecting heteroscedasticity in u_{it} leads to biased inefficiency estimates. Thus, inefficiency determinants of European regions are introduced as shown in the following equation:

For model A:

$$\sigma_{it}^2 = \exp(\gamma_0 + \gamma_1 agri\_pat_{it-2} + \gamma_2 bio\_pat_{it-2} + \varepsilon_{it}) \tag{2.5}$$

For model B:

$$\sigma_{it}^2 = \exp(\gamma_0 + \gamma_1 agri\_pat\_inhab_{it-2} + \gamma_2 bio\_pat\_inhab_{it-2} + \varepsilon_{it}) \tag{2.6}$$

where $agri\_pat_{it-2}$ is the number of agricultural patents, bio_pat_{it-2} is the number of biotechnology patents, $agri\_pat\_inhab_{it-2}$ is the number of agricultural patents per millions of inhabitants and $bio\_pat\_inhab_{it-2}$ is the number of biotechnology patents per millions of inhabitants. Following Yin et al. (2015), we consider a hysteric period for the incorporation of patents within final products, so we take two-year lags of patent variables.

Following Farrell (1957)'s definitions, the technical efficiency of the *i-th* region in the *t-th* time period is estimated by using the conditional mean of the inefficiency term $E\{\exp(-u_{it}|\varepsilon_{it})\}$ proposed by Battese and Coelli (1988) and is given by:

$$TE_{it} = e^{(-u_{it})} = e^{\left(-z_{it}^{'}\gamma - \varepsilon_{it}\right)} \tag{2.7}$$

According to this formula, the technical inefficiency values oscillate between 0 and 1, being the latter the most favourable case. Technical efficiency refers to the ability to obtain maximum output from a given input vector. If $TE_{it} < 1$ then the observable output is less than the maximum feasible output, meaning that the statistical unit is not efficient. After computing technical inefficiency, we are able to rank regions from the least to the most efficient and to find which countries are on average the most efficient.

2.4 Empirical Results

To estimate simultaneously the production stochastic frontier parameters and the inefficiency model coefficients, the maximum-likelihood method is applied to the regional unbalanced dataset of the three European countries considered. In (Table 2.2), alongside the columns the results for three different model specifications—Pitt and Lee (1981), TRE without inefficiency determinants (Greene 2005), TRE with inefficiency determinants—are reported, while alongside the rows, variables of production function model and those of the inefficiency model are presented. At the bottom of (Table 2.2), a Theta parameter is also introduced. It represents the standard deviation of the unobserved heterogeneity(α_i) (Greene, 2005). Therefore, it may be interpreted as the region-specific heterogeneity which is randomly distributed. The statistical significance of this parameter confirms that the TRE model is the most appropriate with respect to the Pitt and Lee model because it allows us to disentangle the unobserved region-specific heterogeneity from the standard error.

For robustness check, we compare these three specifications according to the patent indicators used. In model A, we include the two-year lagged variable of the number of agricultural or biotechnology patent applications while in model B, we consider the two-year lagged variable of the number per millions of inhabitants of agricultural or biotechnology patents.

The estimated Cobb–Douglas stochastic production function coefficients are stable across models and conformed to our expectations. As predicted, all the inputs contribute positively to the representative farmer output in line with the established literature (Tasnim et al., 2015; Auci and Coromaldi, 2021).

The estimated coefficient values of capital, material, and paid labour are positive and statistically significant at the 1% level. This suggests that all the inputs are productive. There exists an opportunity of increasing farming output by enhancing total assets, operating costs, and paid employees. As regards farm size coefficients, they are positive but statistically significant at only the 10% level. This means that the larger the farm, the higher is its farming output because of the economies of scale.

Concerning the patent indicators, the discussion of the results depends on the model used. The first two specifications of model A—Pitt and Lee (1981) and the TRE without inefficiency determinants (Greene 2005)—show positive and statistically significant coefficients of agricultural and biotechnology indicators, expressed in number. Based on a direct relationship between innovation output and firm performance, as in Weerawardena et al. (2006), we found that innovation is a productive factor for enhancing the total output sold of European farmers. In model B, the Pitt and Lee (1981) model shows coefficients with a statistically low level of significance, except for the coefficient related to per millions of inhabitant agricultural patents. Furthermore, the TRE without inefficiency determinants (Greene 2005) specification confirms the positive impact of the agricultural and biotechnology indicators as expressed in number per inhabitant. This result is in line with our expectations. The TRE model even if not including the inefficiency determinants consider explicitly the unobserved heterogeneity disentangling the effect of unmeasured factors from the efficiency.

However, as underlined by Cruz-Cázares et al. (2013), farm performance is influenced through the efficiency with which the innovation process is undertaken. In fact, the desirable innovation process output, such as patents, is related to the efficient use of farm internal capabilities. For this reason, in the TRE model with inefficiency determinants, patent indicators are included inside the inefficiency function as the main factors. As highlighted in the second panel of Table 2.2, the inefficiency components show a negative and statistically significant coefficient, except for the number of agricultural patents per inhabitant. This implies that an increase in the innovation output reduces technical inefficiency and as consequence enhances the regional farming outcome. Moreover, when the regional size is considered, the whole effect of innovation on efficiency is captured by the biotechnology patent indicator.

In Table 2.3, technical efficiency scores of the TRE with inefficiency determinants are shown. As underlined above, the choice of using model 3 depends on the fact that it allows us to disentangle unobserved heterogeneity from the inefficiency effect and to capture the innovation process through the inefficiency specification. In Table 2.3, technical efficiency mean values of European regional farms are reported distinguishing

Table 2.2 Stochastic frontier estimation results for model A and model B based on three different specifications

	Model A			*Model B*		
	(1) Pitt and Lee (1981)	(2) TRE without inefficiency determinants (Greene 2005)	(3) TRE with inefficiency determinants	(1) Pitt and Lee (1981)	(2) TRE without inefficiency determinants (Greene 2005)	(3) TRE with inefficiency determinants
	Production function					
Capital	0.183***	0.137**	0.153***	0.180***	0.132***	0.142**
	(0.004)	(0.015)	(0.006)	(0.008)	(0.009)	(0.026)
Materials	0.451***	0.502***	0.495***	0.456***	0.504***	0.499***
	(0.000)	(0.000)	(0.000)	(0.000)	(0.000)	(0.000)
Unpaid Labour	0.0462	0.059	0.0613	0.042	0.062	0.060
	(0.552)	(0.383)	(0.465)	(0.625)	(0.32)	(0.543)
Paid Labour	0.126***	0.105***	0.106***	0.125***	0.106***	0.109***
	(0.000)	(0.005)	(0.004)	(0.000)	(0.000)	(0.000)
Farm size	0.146*	0.148*	0.136*	0.145*	0.151	0.156*
	(0.075)	(0.052)	(0.070)	(0.095)	(0.116)	(0.059)
Agricultural patent	0.002***	0.003***				
	(0.000)	(0.000)				
Biotechnology patent	0.001**	0.002***				
	(0.018)	(0.001)				
Agricultural patent_inhab				0.002	0.003***	
				(0.255)	(0.000)	

	Model A			*Model B*		
Biotechnology patent_inab				0.003*	0.006***	
				(0.052)	(0.002)	
Constant	1.848***	1.585***	1.674**	1.849***	1.594***	1.558***
	(0.000)	(0.002)	(0.013)	(0.000)	(0.000)	(0.000)
	Inefficiency model					
Agricultural patent			−0.244**			
			(0.020)			
Biotechnology patent			−0.144*			
			(0.059)			
Agricultural patent per inhabitant						−0.525
						(0.247)
Biotechnology patent per inhabitant						−1.903***
						(0.000)
Constant	0.096***	−105.3**	-4.506***	0.0904***	−106.8**	-4.439***
	(0.000)	(0.017)	(0.000)	(0.000)	(0.020)	(0.000)
Observations	480	480	480	480	480	480
N. of regions	58	58	58	58	58	58
Teta		0.143***	0.135***		0.139***	0.132***
Log-likelihood	443.401	450.898	449.80	440.665	446.009	448.297

Note Robust standard errors are clustered at the country level. All explanatory variables are expressed in logarithms except for patent indicators that are lagged by two years. P-values in parentheses. * Significant at 10%; ** significant at 5%; *** significant at 1%

Table 2.3 Technical inefficiency scores by countries

True random effects model with inefficiency determinants (Model A)		*True random effects model with inefficiency determinants (Model B)*	
Country	**Mean efficiency**	**Country**	**Mean efficiency**
France	0.981	**France**	0.994
Italy	0.955	**Italy**	0.983
Spain	0.939	**Spain**	0.972
ANOVA test			
F	54.59***		39.16***
Prob > F	(0.000)		(0.000)

Note p-value in parentheses. * Significant at 10%; ** significant at 5%; *** significant at 1%

between models A and B. The mean efficiency scores in the three countries are very high, ranging from 0.94 to 0.99. This means that the selected countries reveal the existence of a negligible distance to the optimal frontier and specifically farmers residing in the French regions are the most efficient with respect to the Italian and Spanish ones. This result is in line with that found by Auci et al., 2021. The authors find that agricultural firms in northern Europe are more efficient than agricultural firms in southern Europe.

A test on the statistical significance of the difference among regions' mean values is also reported. The analysis of variance (ANOVA), based on ex-post technical inefficiency scores, allows the comparison of the estimated country technical inefficiency means, by testing the mean difference. Thus, the rejection of the null hypothesis confirms that European regions' technical efficiency mean values are statistically different among them. Our results confirm a heterogeneity among European countries in terms of technical efficiency.

The level of French farms' technical efficiencies is higher and remains stable over time as shown in (Fig. 2.1). Conversely, for Italy and Spain, the trend of the scores is more unsteady, especially since the economic crisis of 2008. Thus, French regions are confirmed as those with the most efficient farmers, while Italian and Spanish regions show that farmers have suffered during the second to last economic crisis. This could be partially explained by the fact that countries with a superior innovation capacity are more likely to be able to cope with any kind of crisis, including the economic one. This leaves space for policymakers to intervene in order to increase efficiency through choosing innovation-enhancing policies in the

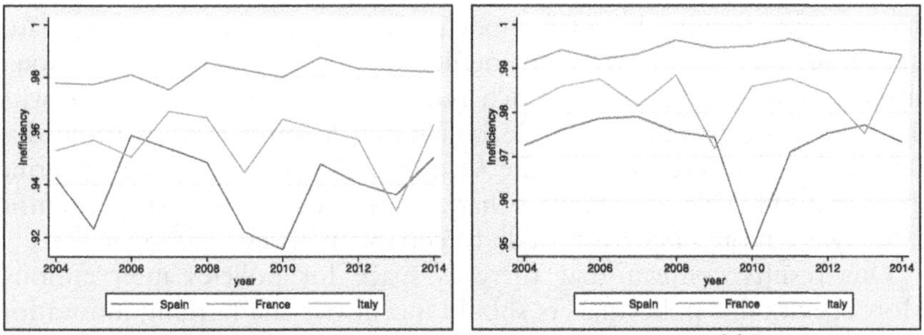

Model A *Model B*

Fig. 2.1 Inefficiency trend by country based on TRE with inefficiency model (Model A) (*Source* Our elaboration)

agricultural sector. Especially considering that this sector will be severely affected by the effects of climate change in the coming years.

2.5 Conclusions

Innovation is a crucial strategy for climate adaptation and a fundamental impulse for agricultural growth. The negative effects of climate change on the European agricultural sector have created a wide consensus on the strategies to be adopted, but a better understanding of farmers' innovative capacity in enhancing the regional farming outcome is needed.

This paper contributes to the innovation-firm performance relationship literature in a threefold way. First, we use FADN the unique source of harmonised micro-economic data on accounting and structural European farms. Second, we analyse innovation outputs (agricultural and biotechnology patents) as determinants of European farmers' efficiency by distinguishing between unobserved heterogeneity and technical efficiency. Third, we estimate the technical efficiency scores of a representative farm at the regional level in the period 2004–2012 by comparing a time-invariant inefficiency model with two different specifications of the time-varying inefficiency model.

The empirical analysis provides two main findings. First, Pitt and Lee (1981) and the TRE without inefficiency determinants (Greene 2005) show positive and statistically significant coefficients of agricultural and biotechnology indicators in both models. Including the inefficiency determinants within the TRE model, results show that a negative and statistically significant effect on inefficiency term enhances the regional farming outcome. Second, French regions are confirmed as those with the most efficient farmers, while Italian and Spanish regions show that farmers have suffered during the second to last economic crisis during the year 2008. This corroborates that countries with a superior innovation capacity are more likely to be able to cope with crises.

Our results confirm that there is space for policies interventions. More specifically, policymakers should incentivise the farming innovation process and farmer output efficiency. Thus, it becomes of primary value to adequately measure farmers' efficiency of technological innovation. This allows policymakers to assess how farmers are developing the innovation process, central to their business success. Technical efficiency analysis shows how positive in terms of performance is an increase in farmers' efficiency due to the innovation process output. As a consequence, farmers should continuously follow the path of a technological innovation process in order to increase their profitability.

References

Agrawala, S., Bordier C., Schreitter V. & Karplus V., (2012), Adaptation and Innovation: An Analysis of Crop Biotechnology Patent Data, OECD Environment WorkingPapers, No. 40, OECD Publishing.

Aigner, D.J., Lovell, C.A.K. & Schmidt, P. (1977). Formulation and estimation of stochastic frontier production function models. *Journal of Econometrics*, 6, 21–37.

Arundel, A. & I. Kabla (1998), "What Percentage of Innovations are Patented? Empirical Estimates for European Firms", *Research Policy* 27, 127–141.

Auci, S., & Coromaldi, M. (2021). Climate variability and agricultural production efficiency: evidence from Ethiopian farmers. *International Journal of Environmental Studies*, 78(1), 57–76.

Auci, S., Barbieri, N., Coromaldi, M., & Vignani, D. (2021). Innovation for climate change adaptation and technical efficiency: an empirical analysis in the European agricultural sector. *Economia Politica*, 38(2), 597–623.

Battese, G., & Coelli, T. (1988). Prediction of firm-level technical efficiencies with a generalized frontier production function and panel data. *Journal of Econometrics*, 38, 387–399.

Belotti, F., Daidone, S., Ilardi, G., & Atella, V. (2013). Stochastic frontier analysis using Stata. *The Stata Journal*, 13(4), 719–758.

Brock, G., & Ogloblin, C. (2014). Another look at technical efficiency in American states, 1979–2000. *The Annals of Regional Science*, 53(2), 577-590.

Cruz-Cázares, C., Bayona-Sáez, C., & García-Marco, T. (2013). You can't manage right what you cant measure well: Technological innovation efficiency. Research Policy, 42(6-7), 1239–1250.

Dechezleprêtre, A., Glachant, M., Haščič, I., Johnstone, N., & Ménière, Y. (2011). Invention and transfer of climate change–mitigation technologies: a global analysis. Review of environmental economics and policy, 5(1), 109–130.

ECONADPT (2016), Results of the ECONADAPT project. Published by the ECONADAPT consortium EEA, European Environment Agency, (2015). *Agriculture and Climate Change.*

EEA, European Environmental Agency (2019). Climate Change Adaptation in the Agriculture Sector in Europe. EEA Report N4–2019. ISSN 1977–8449. https://www.eea.europa.eu/publications/cc-adaptation-agriculture#tab-figures-used

Farrell, M.J. (1957). The measurement of productive efficiency. *Journal of the Royal Statistical Society*, 120(3), 253–281.

Goubanova K. & Li L., (2007), "Extremes in temperature and precipitation around the Mediterranean basin in an ensemble of future climate scenario simulations", *Global and Planetary Change*, 57(1–2), 27–42.

Greene, W. 2005. Reconsidering heterogeneity in panel data estimators of the stochastic frontier model. *Journal of Econometrics* 126: 269–303.

Greene, W.H., 2008. The Econometric Approach to Efficiency Analysis. In H.O. Fried, C.A. Lovell, and S.S. Schmidt (Eds), *The Measurement of Productive Efficiency and Productivity Change*. Oxford: Oxford University Press.

Griliches, Z. & Pakes, A., (1980). Patents and R&D at the firm level: A first report. *Economics Letters*, 5(4), 377–381.

Groombridge, B. (ed.) (1992), "Intellectual Property Rights for Biotechnology", *Global Biodiversity: Status of the Earth's Living Resources*, Chapman and Hall, London, 495–499.

Hadri, K., Guermat, C., & Whittaker, J., (2003). Estimation of technical inefficiency effects using panel data and doubly heteroscedastic stochastic production frontiers. *Empirical Economics*, 28(1), 203–222.

IPCC, (2014), "Climate Change 2014: Impacts, Adaptation, and Vulnerability", Contribution of WGI to the 5th Assessment Report of the IPCC, Geneva.

Janger, J., Schubert, T., Andries, P., Rammer, C., & Hoskens, M. (2017). The EU 2020 innovation indicator: A step forward in measuring innovation outputs and outcomes? *Research Policy*, 46(1), 30–42.

Jonasson, L., & Apland, J., (1997), Programming sector models: Frontier Technology and Inefficiency, *European Review of Agricultural Economics*, 24(1), 109–131.

Maietta, O. W., De Devitiis, B., Destefanis, S., & Suppa, D. (2019). Human capital and rural development policy: evidence from European FADN regions. *Bio-based and Applied Economics*, 8(3), 239–259.

Meeusen, W., & van den Broeck, J. (1977). Efficiency estimation from Cobb-Douglas production functions with composed error. *International Economic Review*, 18, 435–44.

Méon, P.G., & Weill, L. (2005). Does better governance foster efficiency? An aggregate frontier analysis. *Economics of Governance*, 6(1), 75–90.

Méon, P.G., & Weill, L. (2010). Is Corruption an Efficient Grease? *World Development*, 38(3), 244–259.

Méon, P.G., Schneider, F., & Weill, L. (2011). Does taking the shadow economy into account matter when measuring aggregate efficiency? *Applied Economics*, 43(18), 2303–2311.

Moroney, J., & Lovell, C.A.K. (1997). The relative efficiencies of market and planned economies. *Southern Economic Journal*, 63(4), 1084–1093.

Nelson, R. R. (1991). Why do firms differ, and how does it matter? *Strategic Management Journal*, 12(S2), 61–74.

Pitt, M. M., & Lee, L. F. (1981). The measurement and sources of technical inefficiency in the Indonesian weaving industry. *Journal of Development Economics*, 9(1), 43–64.

Popp, D. (2005) Lessons from patents: using patents to measure technological change in environmental models. *Ecological Economics*, 54(2), 209–226.

Rodriguez Diaz, J.A., Weatherhead, E.K., Knox, J.W., & Camacho, E. (2007), "Climate change impacts on irrigation water requirements in the Guadalquivir River basin in Spain", *Regional Environmental Change* 7, 149–159.

Su, H. N., & Moaniba, I. M. (2017). Does innovation respond to climate change? Empirical evidence from patents and greenhouse gas emissions. *Technological Forecasting and Social Change* 122, 49-62

Tasnim, Z., Hafeez, A. G., & Majumder, S. (2015). Climate change and wheat production in drought prone areas of Bangladesh-A technical efficiency analysis. *Journal of Agricultural Science*, 7(1), 43.

Vanschoenwinkela J., R. Mendelsohn, & Van Passel S. (2017). Do Western and Eastern Europe have the same agricultural climate response? Taking adaptive capacity into account. *Global Environmental Change*, 41 (2016) 74–87 C.

Weerawardena, J., O'Cass, A., & Julia, C., 2006. Does industry matter? Examining the role of industry structure and organizational learning in innovation and brand performance. *Journal of Business Research* 59, 37–45.

Yin, J., Zheng, M., & Chen, J. (2015). The effects of environmental regulation and technical progress on CO2 Kuznets curve: An evidence from China. *Energy Policy* 77, 97–108.

Zilberman D., Lipper L., McCarthy N., & Gordon B. (2018). "Innovation in Response to Climate Change". In: Lipper L., McCarthy N., Zilberman D., Asfaw S., Branca G. (eds) *Climate Smart Agriculture. Natural Resource Management and Policy*, 52. Springer, Cham.

CHAPTER 3

The Role of Innovation in Sustainable Cocoa Cultivation: Moving Beyond Mitigation and Adaptation

Sylvester Afram Boadi, Mette Fog Olwig, Richard Asare, Aske Skovmand Bosselmann, and Kwadwo Owusu

Abstract Cocoa cultivation is both severely threatened by climate change and a potential contributor to climate change through deforestation. Based on a review of the literature and secondary documents, as well as field observations and interviews, this chapter examines different innovations in Ghana's cocoa sector, the ways in which they aim to address

S. A. Boadi · K. Owusu
Department of Geography and Resource Development, University of Ghana, Legon, Ghana
e-mail: safram_boadi@st.ug.edu.gh

K. Owusu
e-mail: kowusu@ug.edu.gh

M. F. Olwig (✉)
Department of Social Sciences and Business, Roskilde University, Roskilde, Denmark
e-mail: mettefo@ruc.dk

M. Coromaldi and S. Auci (eds.), *Climate-Induced Innovation*,
https://doi.org/10.1007/978-3-031-01330-0_3

sustainable cocoa cultivation, and the challenges to their adoption. We find that cocoa farmers are generally open to innovation and new technology. Yet, while farmers respond positively to certain innovations, they do not fully adopt others. This uneven adoption, we argue, is not just a result of limited resources or poor extension services but stems from a failure to address the multiple challenges farmers face when introducing new innovations, including insecure land-use rights, youth disinterest, migration, and seemingly lucrative alternative land use. While promising innovations, such as agroforestry and smartphone applications for agricultural service delivery and training, are currently being implemented, such innovations, we conclude, will only lead to sustainable cocoa cultivation if these broader challenges are addressed, thereby moving beyond a narrower concern with yields and climate change mitigation and adaptation.

Keywords Agricultural innovation · Cocoa systems · Sustainable agriculture · Mitigation · Adaptation · Climate change

3.1 Introduction

Climate change is affecting several productive sectors around the world, especially climate sensitive sectors like agriculture and forestry (IPCC, 2014). In Ghana, rainfall and temperatures have already been impacted and even more dramatic changes, posing severe risks for cocoa production, are expected in the future. The cocoa tree is sensitive to climatic factors, including floods, drought, and high temperatures. Yet, cocoa cultivation is also alleged to be a contributor to climate change because

R. Asare
International Institute of Tropical Agriculture, Accra, Ghana
e-mail: r.asare@cgiar.org

A. S. Bosselmann
Department of Food and Resource Economics, University of Copenhagen, Frederiksberg, Denmark
e-mail: ab@ifro.ku.dk

the global increase in the demand for cocoa beans has driven the expansion of cocoa cultivation further into forested land. The negative consequences of such expansionist practices include degradation of forestlands, deforestation, and loss of biodiversity (Nunoo et al., 2015). These expansion measures have characterized all cocoa producing countries but there are differences in yields, national outputs, and thereby environmental impacts, between producing countries. Cote d'Ivoire, Ghana, and Indonesia have some of the highest cocoa-driven deforestation impacts, with Cote d'Ivoire presenting an extreme case of both the rates and impacts of biodiversity loss associated with cocoa expansion efforts in recent decades (Barima et al., 2016; Ongolo et al., 2018). Producing countries in Latin America, on the other hand, are generally associated with lower environmental footprints except for Peru, where large-scale clearing of forests for industrial cocoa cultivation poses a challenge to the Amazon Forest (Kroeger et al., 2017).

Differences in yields are partly explained by differences in farm ownership and farm sizes. Cocoa farming is a tropical agricultural activity, and smallholder farmers form the majority of cocoa producers worldwide (Mondelēz International, 2015). Large-scale plantations in the Americas and Asia contribute only a small proportion of the world's cocoa production (World Cocoa Foundation, 2014), but have high yields with more well-resourced owners. In Africa, the bulk of the smallholder cocoa producing households cultivate less than 2 hectares and farmers lack access to agricultural inputs, such as fertilizers and pesticides, credit, and quality planting material (World Cocoa Foundation, 2014; Hutchins et al., 2015). Differences in yields are furthermore often attributed to productive efficiency and adoption of innovation and technology (Meijer et al., 2015). According to Aneani et al. (2011), farmers across the cocoa regions in Ghana have a potential yield of about 1000 kg/ha or more, however, the actual yield since 2012 is around 500 kg/ha (FAOSTAT, 2020). Successive governments and research institutions have therefore introduced cocoa farmers to various innovations, practices, and technologies aimed at closing this deficit (Abdulai et al., 2020). In Ghana, cocoa farmers are generally open to innovation and new technology, yet, while farmers respond positively to certain innovations, they do not fully adopt other innovations (Aneani et al., 2011). Important reasons for this are that farmers lack the resources to adopt and sustain these practices and that the effective implementation of policies, technologies, and innovations depends on an efficient extension service sector—a sector which is underdeveloped in Ghana (Gockowski et al., 2011; Bell et al., 2013). By examining different innovations in Ghana's cocoa sector, the ways in which they aim to address sustainable cocoa cultivation, and the challenges to their adoption, this chapter further illuminates the multiple challenges that hinder farmers' adoption of innovations, including insecure land-use rights, youth disinterest and migration as well as seemingly lucrative competing alternative land uses.

Promising innovations are being introduced in cocoa farming, such as Agroforestry Systems and Information and Communication Technology (ICT)-based services. A growing body of literature emphasizes that agroforestry systems can support mitigation and adaptation efforts, thereby both addressing the impact of cocoa production on climate change and climate change impacts on cocoa production (Dagar & Tewari, 2017). ICT-based services, on the other hand, respond to the challenges of low agricultural extension coverage by providing a platform for instantaneously delivering time-sensitive information, such as good agricultural practices and weather-related farming recommendations, which is even more critical now because of changing rainfall and temperature conditions. These new innovations are implemented largely by profit-driven private sector companies in the cocoa value chain, especially large cocoa trading and chocolate manufacturing companies that have access to resources and advanced technology. Yet these companies cannot easily address challenges that pertain to land rights and alternative land use. The chapter concludes that new innovations could be key to sustainable cocoa cultivation, but only if there is a move beyond a narrow focus on yields and climate change mitigation/adaptation and toward a concern with broader challenges.

The following sections will first provide background, methods, and conceptual definitions, and then present the different innovations that have been introduced in the Ghanaian cocoa sector over time in order to analyze the diverse barriers farmers experience in implementing new innovations that could potentially secure future cocoa production in Ghana.

3.2 Background, Methods, and Conceptual Definitions

Background

Ghana's cocoa producing regions have significant differences in output. After cocoa was gradually introduced and adopted by smallholder farmers in Ghana in the nineteenth century, production has been influenced by the availability of forestlands for farm expansion, pest and disease outbreaks, climate variability and change, access to new and improved planting materials, the availability of labor (Kolavalli & Vigneri, 2011) and colonial and post-colonial government policy (Kolavalli & Vigneri, 2017). These factors have contributed to fluctuations in national output and to the geographic spread of cultivation from the Eastern Region to Ashanti, Brong-Ahafo, Central, Volta, and Western regions (see Fig. 3.1).

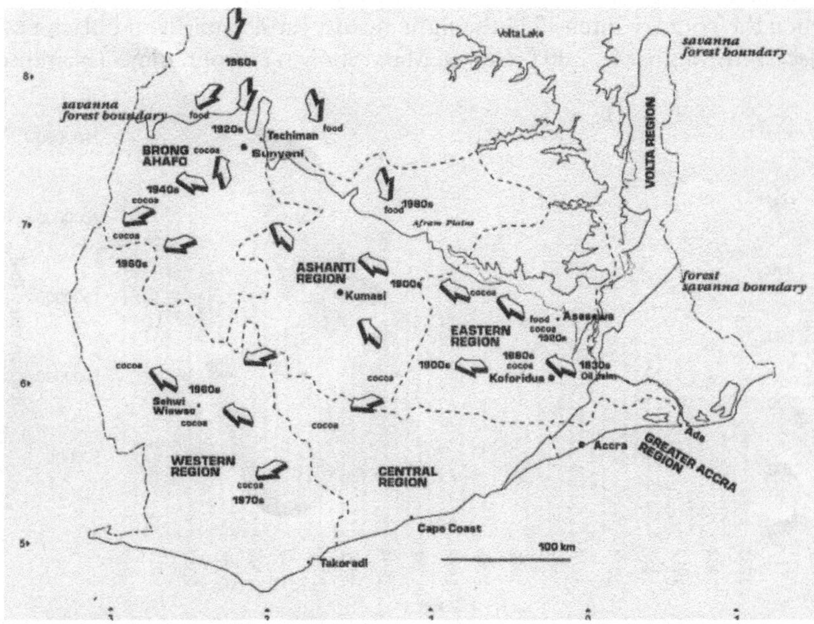

Fig. 3.1 Geographic spread of cocoa farming from the Eastern to Western regions in Ghana (*Source* Amanor [1996])

In the early 1980s, overall cocoa output fell significantly across all the Ghanaian cocoa producing regions (see Fig. 3.2), reaching a low of 159,000 metric tons. This was mainly a result of a period of severe drought and bushfires associated with El Niño, which led to the loss of cocoa farms (Kolavalli & Vigneri, 2011). The government responded by investing in new and early maturing cocoa varieties that were adapted to growing under less shade and encouraging farmers to shift to zero shade (full sun) cocoa systems (Gockowski et al., 2013). In the decades that followed, cocoa cultivation went through two expansion waves: extensive cultivation in the late 1990s, then intensive cultivation in the 2000s due to government policy direction and land scarcity (Gockowski et al., 2011).

In the first phase, the annual rate of expansion was high and occurred on primary forestlands in the Western Region between 1990 and 1999 (Gockowski et al., 2011). Nevertheless, farmers' output per hectare kept declining and significant yield increases only occurred in the second phase when the country intensified the fight against capsid/mirid and black pod disease through the 2001 Cocoa Mass Spraying Programme (Naminse

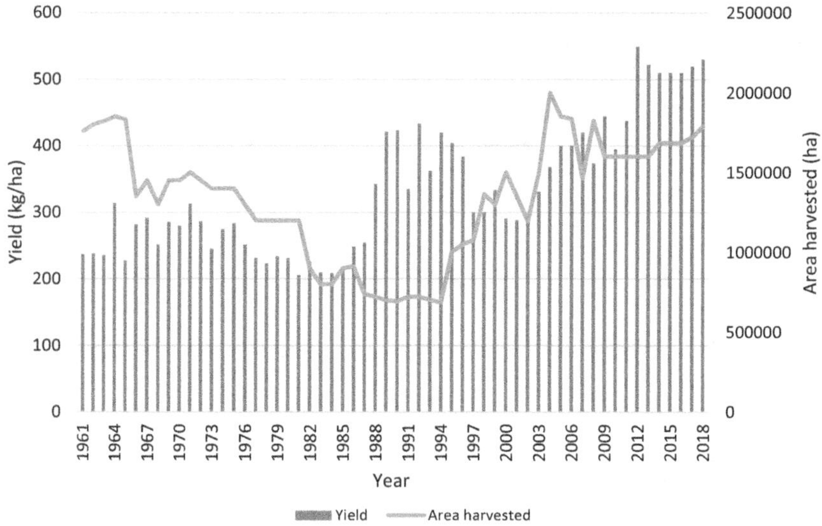

Fig. 3.2 Cocoa productivity and area cultivated in Ghana, 1961 to 2018 (*Source* Based on Data from FAOSTAT [2020])

et al., 2011), and implemented the Cocoa Hi-Tech Programme (the distribution of subsidized fertilizers for use by farmers) in 2002/2003 (Kolavalli & Vigneri, 2017). These programs aimed at shifting cocoa cultivation from extensive low inputs to intensive cultivation using modern cultivation practices and scientific techniques. As a result, production grew from about 400,000 metric tons in the 1990s (Dormon et al., 2004) to more than 700,000 metric tons in the 2003/2004 season (Naminse et al., 2011) reaching a peak output of 1 million metric tons in 2010/2011 (Aneani et al., 2011; Hutchins et al., 2015). Since this milestone output, the national production has oscillated between 740,000 and 970,000 metric tons, but the 2020/2021 season hit the 1 million tons mark again (COCOBOD, 2021). The recovery of the national cocoa bean output since the 1990s, after the near collapse of the sector in the early 1980s, also coincided with a slightly higher rainfall phase of the decadal and multi-decadal variability in the West African rainfall regime (Rodríguez-Fonseca et al., 2011). The growth of Ghana's national cocoa output could therefore be attributed to increases in the total land under cultivation, a series of supportive governmental policies and intensification programs, and favorable rainfall.

The overall cocoa productivity for the last decade (2010–2019) has been at an all-time high (see Fig. 3.2) and has thus improved compared to pre-2000 levels. The current yield of 500 kg/ha is, however, still significantly lower than in other regions of the world. For example, cocoa yields are about 655 kg/ha in Indonesia (Fahmid et al., 2018), 650 kg/ha in Peru (Scott et al., 2016), and 600 kg/ha in Cote d'Ivoire (Cobbina, 2014). Furthermore, the current yield increase is largely due to the abandonment of less productive plots and significant increases in the establishment of plots in new frontiers, especially when compared to the late 1980s and early 1990s (Fig. 3.2). Cocoa cultivation is therefore seen as a major culprit in primary forest loss and overall deforestation in Ghana (Asare, 2019).

Ghana's cocoa producing regions have been projected to be affected negatively by climate changes (Bunn et al., 2019) in part because cocoa production is mainly done on a rain-fed basis (UNDP, 2012) and irrigated cocoa fields are basically non-existent (Stanturf et al., 2011). Rainfall is observed to have declined by 20% compared to pre-1970s levels in the cultivated forest zones of the country (Owusu & Waylen, 2009), while many climate projections for the country point to a warmer dry climate in the future across most agro-ecological zones (McSweeney et al., 2010;

Amlalo & Oppong-Boadi, 2015). For instance, projections show mean annual temperature increases of 1.2 °C by 2030 and 2.1 °C by 2050 for the cocoa belt in general (Läderach et al., 2013). Läderach et al. (2013) argue that increased evapotranspiration resulting from these projected temperature increases would pose significant risk to cocoa, which is a drought sensitive crop.

Bunn et al. (2019) have identified four agro-climatic zones with different suitability levels for cocoa production now and in the future. Zone 1, corresponding to the Southern Bono and Ahafo Regions, is characterized by very long dry seasons, a higher number of dry months and low rainfall. These conditions worsen under future projections and the entire Zone 1 is predicted to become unsuitable for cocoa cultivation. Zone 2, associated with the Ashanti Region, has a long dry season, low temperatures, and average rainfall and future suitability is classified as uncertain. Zone 3, covering areas in the Eastern Region, has high temperatures in the dry months, an even distribution of rainfall throughout the year with low seasonal variations. Future suitability for Zone 3 shows a mix of suitable, uncertain, and unsuitable areas. Zone 4, coinciding with the southern growing belts in the Western, Western North, and Central Regions, is associated with a brief dry season and high annual rainfall. Future projections show uncertain changes in the northern parts of these regions and a small reduction in suitability levels for cocoa production.

These suitability changes coupled with other climatic and non-climatic stressors will likely result in severe livelihood losses for cocoa farmers. The general lack of crop insurance, efficient technology and financial and physical infrastructure severely reduce the cocoa farmers' ability to limit climate change impacts or to move their production to the new areas projected to be suitable for cocoa cultivation (McKinley et al., 2016; Bunn et al., 2019; Läderach et al., 2013).

Methods

This study is based on review and analysis of literature on cocoa production in Ghana, supplemented by field research. The literature search was conducted on SCOPUS, Web of Science, Google Scholar, and Google web search covering research publications from the 1980s to 2019. They included peer-reviewed journal articles, book series, conference proceedings, theses, and organizational reports on cocoa systems, innovation adoption, the use of technology, climate change in Ghana's cocoa sector, and sustainability issues. The initial search produced over 60 key publications, 30 of which were selected for further review. The final selection of literature was based on whether the study in question discussed two or more of the following: agricultural innovation, cocoa cultivation practices, technology and the cocoa sector, climate change, extension services, cocoa farmer adaptation, and cocoa sustainability initiatives. In addition, historical data on Ghana's cocoa bean output, productivity/yield, and area harvested were downloaded from FAOSTAT. Field research took place as part of the Danida-funded Climate-smart cocoa systems for Ghana (CLIMCOCOA) project. It comprised field observations, interviews, and discussions from field visitations, 402 household surveys and 20 focused group discussions conducted from February to May 2019 in 12 cocoa communities across the Ashanti, Ahafo, Western, and Western North Regions.

The Concept of Innovation in the Context of Climate Change

Innovation in an agricultural value chain is crucial for managing production and for reducing both environmental and non-environmental shocks and stresses. We conceptualize agricultural innovation as the introduction of new or existing products (e.g., agricultural inputs), processes (e.g., practices of cultivation, marketing), or ways of organization (e.g., institutions and policies) with the goal of increasing efficiency, competitiveness, effectiveness, resilience, and sustainability (FAO, 2018; Munthali et al., 2018). Importantly, innovation is thereby more than just the development of technology, tools and farm machinery, and improved practices. It also involves creating supportive institutions and stakeholder networks, and policies, which are critical to developing, using, and sharing agricultural knowledge and information (FAO, 2018).

Even though the social and institutional context is critical for shaping people's perception of, and ability to deal with, environmental challenges, innovation in the context of climate change mitigation and adaptation initiatives tends to be dominated by technocratic and technological approaches (Rodima-Taylor et al., 2012; Olwig, 2012). Those in power prefer focusing on the development of new technology because "[c]hanging social and economic factors usually means altering the way that power operates in a society" (Wisner et al., 2004: 7). Such changes could for example entail land reform, land-use restrictions, or investments in infrastructure in poor regions, changes that are both expensive and likely to face powerful political opposition (ibid.). In the context of cocoa farming, as will be further discussed below, social factors that influence the types of challenges that actors face include demographic factors such as resource endowments, level of education, extent of income diversification, age, and gender (Ali et al., 2018; Djokoto et al., 2016).

3.3 Innovation and Cocoa Cultivation: Possibilities and Challenges

International and local research efforts generally focus on innovations that aim to protect both cocoa farmers' livelihood assets and the environment. Full sun cocoa systems and new and improved seed varieties were among the first innovations introduced to Ghanaian cocoa farmers. However, because of the mounting global concern with the environment and climate change, new areas of research concern the role of innovations such as cocoa agroforestry systems (e.g., Nunoo & Owusu, 2017) and voluntary sustainability standards (VSS)/certification schemes (Fenger et al., 2017; Ingram et al. 2018; Uribe-Leitz & Ruf, 2019) for improving cocoa farmers' incomes and developing a sustainable cocoa sector. In addition to these, most licensed cocoa buying companies and several international NGOs are currently developing cocoa sustainability initiatives and projects that introduce innovations as a way of demonstrating their sustainability goals/objectives and, as argued by some studies, to better control sustainability narratives to consumers (Odijie, 2018). Table 3.1 highlights some of these initiatives implemented by key companies within Ghana's cocoa value chain.

Another innovation, spearheaded by large trading companies, is the dissemination of agricultural advisory services through smartphone applications (ICT-based services) and the development of service delivery models, which may include training, inputs, and new seedlings (Muilerman & Vellema, 2017; Witteveen et al., 2017). Much as is the case with certification, the aim is to create more viable production systems for the benefit of producers as well as buyers. These different types of innovation present the farmers with a range of opportunities, but the farmers experience several barriers to their adoption. This will be discussed in the following sections which look at new improved planting materials, cocoa agroforestry, organic cocoa farming, VSS, service delivery models, and ICT-based services.

Table 3.1 Sustainability projects of key value chain actors in Ghana

	Company	*Sustainability project(s)*	*Years (start, end)*	*Partners*
1	Solidaridad	Cocoa Rehabilitation and Intensification Programme (CORIP I and II)	2014 up to date	Embassy of the Kingdom of The Netherlands
2	Olam Cocoa	Olam Livelihood Charter (OLC) - Olam Farmer Information System (OFIS), etc	2010 up to date	Bill & Melinda Gates Foundation; IDH (Sustainable Trade Initiative); Rainforest Alliance; USAID
3	ECOM Agroindustrial Corporation Ltd	Sustainable Management Services (SMS)	2012 up to date	International Finance Corporation; FMO; IDH
4	Chocolats Halba/Sunray	Dynamic agroforestry (DAF)/Sankofa project	2016 up to date	Coop Sustainability Fund; Kuapa Kokoo Cooperative; the International Trade Center; Max Havelaar; Fairtrade Africa; WWF; Swiss State Secretariat for Economic Affairs (SECO)
5	Barry Callebaut	Cocoa Horizons	2015 up to date	Barry Callebaut Group
6	Mondelēz International	Cocoa Life	2012 up to date	Barry Callebaut; CARE; Cargill; ECOM; Fairtrade; Jacobs Foundation; Olam; Save the Children; Solidaridad; Swisscontact; VSO; World Vision
7	Hershey	Kakum Cocoa Agroforestry Landscape Program (under the Cocoa for Good strategy)	2019 up to date	ECOM; Ghana's Nature Conservation Research Centre; the Ghana Forestry Commission; the Ghana Cocoa Board (COCOBOD)

(continued)

Table 3.1 (continued)

	Company	*Sustainability project(s)*	*Years (start, end)*	*Partners*
8	Cargill	Cocoa Promise	2012 up to date	CARE; International Cocoa Initiative (ICI)
9	Mars	Cocoa for Generations (under the Sustainable in a Generation Plan)	2018 up to date	CARE; Jacobs Foundation; Bernard van Leer Foundation; UBS Optimus Foundations Foundation
10	Nestlé	Nestlé Cocoa Plan (under the Nestlé's Creating Shared Value [CSV])	2009 up to date	ECOM; International Cocoa Initiative; Cocoanect; Cocoa Merchants
11	World Cocoa Foundation (WCF)	CocoaAction	2014 to date	Barry Callebaut; Blommer Chocolate Company; Cargill; The Ferrero Group; Hershey; Mars; Mondelēz International; Nestlé; Olam International
12	IDH and WCF	Cocoa & Forest Initiative	2017 to date	Governments of Cote d'Ivoire and Ghana, and 35 leading cocoa and chocolate companies

Improved Planting Materials

Cocoa farmers in Ghana employ one of two cocoa planting methods. Some plant at stake using cocoa seeds from their own farms, from the farms of friends or relatives, or from seed gardens, while others use seedlings (hybrid and/or local landrace varieties) transplanted from formal or informal nurseries (Barrientos et al., 2008). In general, there is a low adoption of improved cocoa varieties, and the cultivation of low-quality planting material easily affected by pests and diseases combined with declining soil fertility, and the loss of protective shade for new seedlings have led to high seedling mortality, low yields and difficulties in the establishment of new cocoa farms (Padi et al., 2013; Asare et al., 2016; Aneani & Padi, 2017). Other factors resulting in low-yielding extensive cultivation systems are aged cocoa farms, farmers' lack of capacity to replant old farms, and farmers' reluctance to cut diseased cocoa trees.

Asare et al. (2010) have reported productivity gains of 50% among cocoa producers, who have fully planted improved hybrid cocoa varieties in Ghana, and efforts to increase cocoa yields in West Africa have strongly focused on planting new improved cocoa varieties on old and abandoned cocoa farms (Padi et al., 2013). The low cultivation of improved cocoa varieties is often ascribed to farmers' preference for sourcing seeds/seedlings from old plots or other informal channels, poor access to improved planting materials (Asare et al., 2016), and the reluctance among some farmers to plant these improved varieties (Aneani & Padi, 2017). The Government of Ghana and the Ghana Cocoa Board (COCOBOD) intermittently implement rehabilitation projects when aged cocoa trees and Cocoa Swollen Shoot Virus Disease (CSSVD) begin to pose significant threats to national cocoa outputs. Other local/international organizations have also pursued cocoa rehabilitation initiatives using improved hybrid seedlings through underplanting, gradual replanting, and complete replanting methods. These initiatives include supplying improved seedlings and shade trees to assist farmers to replant their farms (Asare et al., 2018); encouraging farmers to cut down all CSSVD infested trees through paid compensation packages; and providing farmers with support services and training (Kroeger et al., 2017). However, according to field interviews conducted with farmers, COCOBOD personnel must first come and measure the farms to determine the number of seedlings required and the farmers must transport the seedlings from the Seed Production Division (SPD) of COCOBOD at their own expense, creating bottlenecks to these free seedling distribution initiatives. In addition to the regular annual distribution of free hybrid seedlings, successive governments through COCOBOD have implemented specialized programs meant to also raise and distribute free seedlings to farmers. For instance, COCOBOD in 2019 mandated the SPD to raise 60 million hybrid seedlings for free distribution to farmers (Amankwaah et al., 2021). The 2019 program was targeted at farmers, who are replanting their CSSVD infested farms, aiming to rehabilitate old, abandoned, or unproductive farms, or attempting to establish new farms, especially young farmers.

Despite such rehabilitation programs, Gockowski et al. (2011) puts the percentage of cocoa farms cultivated with improved varieties in the Western Region at about 8% of the total bearing acreage. Based on interviews and discussions in the field, farmers still primarily rely on seeds from their farms or from other community members' farms. The improved seeds require adequate nutrients, good distribution of rainfall and the application of pesticides and have a shorter life span due to their high productivity compared to the old variety that produces less, but can manage limited nutrients with shade and has a long rotation period. Hence, the farmers prefer the old varieties in terms of financial investments and returns.

Cocoa Agroforestry Systems

Ghana loses about 2% of its total forestland annually to degradation and deforestation, with cocoa cultivation as one of the major culprits (Amlalo & Oppong-Boadi, 2015; Asare, 2019). As a result, cocoa agroforestry systems are increasingly being explored as viable adaptation and mitigation options for smallholder cocoa farmers in Ghana. Cocoa agroforestry has the potential to serve as forest corridors (Asare et al., 2014) and as buffer zones around protected forest landscapes (Asare, 2005), thus limiting forest fragmentation. They are therefore seen to hold the potential to constitute both a good climate-smart agricultural strategy and a means to improving farmer wealth and resilience (Neufeldt et al., 2009; Alliance for a Green Revolution in Africa [AGRA], 2014).

Cocoa agroforestry is defined as a form of tree diversification, which includes a strategic integration in time and space of suitable and valuable non-cocoa tree species and other plants for agronomic, environmental, and economic benefits (Asare, 2006). Cocoa agroforestry systems help conserve soil moisture, protect agricultural lands from erosion and degradation, enhance on-farm biodiversity, and provide on-farm production diversification avenues (Graefe et al., 2017; Vaast & Somarriba, 2014). Furthermore, the integration of trees in cropping systems also provides smallholder farmers with additional income through the harvest and sale of firewood, fruits, and in some instances, timber (Asare et al., 2014; Graefe et al., 2017). Cocoa farm rehabilitation is also easier and much more possible in shaded systems (Ruf & Schroth, 2004).

Notwithstanding these benefits, not all experts see cocoa agroforestry as an economically viable option for smallholder farmers. A study by Abdulai et al. (2018) found that under extreme drought and heat conditions, some shade trees compete with cocoa for moisture in marginal areas. It concluded that cocoa trees under full sun systems are more resilient to extreme drought than some shaded cocoa systems (ibid.). Gockowski et al. (2013) also argue that intensified full sun production systems make more economic sense in terms of bean production than cocoa agroforestry systems with regard to Ghana's objective of increasing national output. This is because this system would generate higher farmer cocoa incomes (in the short run), while also saving some 200,000 hectares of land as farmers can increase their cocoa yields by adopting intensified full sun systems as opposed to expanding the area under cultivation, thereby avoiding deforestation. However, the monospecific nature of the full sun cocoa systems leads to reduced production diversification, the loss of ecosystem goods and services, and the reduction of tree species and biological diversity on the farm, thereby making the cocoa trees more prone to pests and diseases, shortening the production cycle of cocoa systems, and exhausting soil fertility early (Vaast & Somarriba, 2014; Nunoo & Owusu, 2017; UNDP, 2012). Higher productivity from intensified full sun production systems therefore come with higher investment costs from the increased application of labor, pesticides, and fertilizer to maintain soil fertility (Obiri et al., 2007).

While several projects have introduced cocoa farmers to agroforestry in Ghana, institutional bottlenecks regarding land and tree rights and ownership hinder the implementation of these systems (Proven Ag Solutions, 2014; Roth et al., 2017). Complex land-use rights and a complicated tree rights policy for cocoa farmers conflict with the interests of customary landowners (Roth et al., 2017). Though dominated by smallholder farms, cocoa farming in Ghana comprises different groups with markedly different land rights. Actors engaged in cocoa farming can be categorized hierarchically from the bottom as: hired laborers, sharecroppers/caretakers, farm owners who are primarily farmers, farm owners with non-farm primary occupation but occasional engagement with farming, and farm owners with non-farm primary occupation and no direct engagement with farming. Lowest in the hierarchy are migrants from the northern part of Ghana (although they may be second or third generation migrants), and at the top farm owners, primarily indigenes (Anyidoho et al., 2012). During fieldwork we encountered many instances where land used for cocoa farms had been converted to other uses, e.g., for village-level infrastructure such as new roads or new school buildings, or to other income-generating activities, such as leasing or selling the land. Sometimes, depending on the land-use rights, this is done without the cocoa farmers' consent. At other times, the farmer participates in the decision and benefits from it. In addition to getting an income from the leasing or selling of land to, for example, large-scale gold mining companies, other competing land uses include illegal small-scale gold mining (called "galamsey"). Both forms of gold mining severely degrade the land. As a result, whenever farmers are uncertain about whether they will maintain either their ownership of the land or their user access to it in the foreseeable future, they are discouraged from investing in shade trees, as such trees only provide benefits in the long term. Many farmers instead adopt full sun cocoa systems as they increase yields in the short term and provide economic returns early compared to shaded systems (Franzen & Borgerhoff Mulder, 2007; Nunoo & Owusu, 2017).

Another challenge for agroforestry is that integrating trees into agricultural production systems may engender ecological competition between the trees and crops. Other crops will not do well under dense tree canopies unless they are understory crops/trees. Even for cocoa as an understory crop, several studies have found shade density to reduce yields (Ruf & Schroth, 2004; Gockowski & Sonwa, 2011; Gockowski et al., 2013). Shade trees may also serve as hosts for pests and lead to increased black pod infestation if tree selection, shade management, and pruning are not carefully done (Ruf, 2011; Graefe et al., 2017). Trees in their early maturing stage furthermore pose specific challenges to farmers. Farmers in Western Kenya, for instance, reported not benefitting from trees that are not mature (Thorlakson & Neufeldt, 2012).

The local botanical knowledge possessed by farmers is yet another important factor accounting for cocoa farmers' adoption or non-adoption of cocoa agroforestry systems. Only the indigenes of forest communities tend to know the importance of locally available timber and non-timber forest products (Gockowski et al., 2010). This knowledge is limited among migrant farmers especially because most of them come from a different ecological zone (Ruf & Schroth, 2004). In Ghana for example, migrant farmers from the north might not know the many uses forest community dwellers have for timber and non-timber forest products and may therefore not maintain them on their farms. If the farmers are unaware of the use of forest products, they may not perceive cocoa agroforestry as profitable, and be unwilling to adopt the practice.

Organic Cocoa Farming

Organic farming describes a type of farming which aims at sustaining and enhancing the health of the biomass and improving and maintaining environmental quality through ecological processes and nature-based recycling (Djokoto et al., 2016; Reganold & Wachter, 2016). One of the defining features of organic farming is that no synthetic chemicals are applied. As emphasized by the International Federation of Organic Agriculture Movements [IFOAM] (2010), farmers involved in organic agriculture are not allowed to use agrochemicals such as synthetic fertilizers and pesticides, and genetically modified organisms (GMOs). Organic farming systems also place emphasis on managing pests naturally or biologically, and replenishing soil nutrients by using compost and animal and green manure (Reganold & Wachter, 2016). As climate change issues have brought sustainability issues to the fore of the international debate on agricultural development, such sustainable production methods that increase yields and protect the environment at the same time have become increasingly important to crop production systems (Bandanaa et al., 2016). Organic farming is seen as a climate-smart agricultural practice that relies on ecological and biological components of the environment for production. Such systems are furthermore known to earn premium prices on the international market as markets become increasingly differentiated. Organic cocoa is mostly produced in The Dominican Republic, Belize, and Tanzania (Barrientos et al., 2008). The global market for organic cocoa is small, but expected to grow (Meier et al., 2020). In

2016, for example, organic cocoa comprised only 157,275 metric tons out of about 4.5 million metric tons (Voora et al., 2019).

Organic cocoa farming was introduced in Ghana to improve productivity levels and limit the carbon and environmental footprints of cocoa cultivation systems (Bandanaa et al., 2016). The volume of organic cocoa in Ghana is not significant compared to production from conventional sources (Glin et al., 2015), but Ghana has the potential to expand its organic cocoa component and earn more premium from the growing international market for organic and sustainably produced cocoa beans (Barrientos et al., 2008). Institutional challenges could explain why this potential has not yet been fully exploited with only a few farmers producing organically certified cocoa beans across limited communities in Eastern, Ashanti, and Central regions. Agro Eco-Louis Bolk Institute and Yayra Glover, which are the two major institutions promoting organic cocoa in Ghana, control their own production networks in agreed zones of the country (Glin et al., 2015). The procedure for earning organic certificates and premiums is rigorous (Djokoto et al., 2016). It is therefore not surprising that factors such as not belonging to a farmer-based organization and the limited access to credit, institutional support and services (including both extension services, but also access to organic production inputs) in the cocoa zones, where Agro Eco-Louis Bolk Institute and Yayra Glover are not present to facilitate production, would lead to low diffusion and adoption rates of organic cocoa systems in these zones (Djokoto et al., 2016). Even though organic cocoa cultivation is considered to benefit both the environment and farmers' livelihoods because of the premium prices for organic cocoa, the production and marketing challenges in the organic cocoa network will require significant attention if more farmers are to be attracted to organic cocoa cultivation.

Voluntary Sustainability Standards (VSS)

As already discussed, cocoa cultivation zones have been associated with extensive deforestation and land degradation due to farmers' preference for cultivating new lands rather than rehabilitating old cocoa plots (Clough et al., 2009). The ecological challenges associated with this cocoa-induced deforestation coupled with risks from climate change, and human and social issues such as child labor concerns have generated some international outcry on how cocoa production is organized in producing countries (Ingram et al., 2018; Sadhu et al. 2020). Due to these concerns, companies are under pressure to demonstrate that their cocoa is sourced from producers who grow and process cocoa under sustainable environmental, social, and economic conditions and who protect the well-being of the workers. To achieve set sustainability objectives, companies in the cocoa value chain have relied on VSS offered through certification schemes such as UTZ, Rainforest Alliance, Fairtrade or Organic and through service delivery models (SDM, see below) (Ingram et al., 2018). Certification efforts aim to differentiate markets for agricultural produce and reward agricultural systems that conserve biodiversity and provide other social and environmental benefits (Gockowski et al., 2010). Most of the agricultural products from Africa are consumed in Europe and North America, where some environmental and social quality standards are demanded from the producers (Fenger et al., 2017). Certifications are third-party verification schemes to ensure farmer compliance to these higher standards required by consumers.

Farmers can earn premiums when they sell their certified cocoa beans to Licensed Buying Companies (LBCs) recommended by the certification body or the local organization managing farmers certification license. While premiums are not usually the major benefit farmers gain from certification schemes, they are still important as they tend to motivate farmers to see the need and value of the certification process (Daghela Bisseleua et al., 2013). As part of the certification process, they learn new cultivation practices, benefit from accompanying interventions that improve their natural and financial capital, and enjoy other assets that are not usually provided by LBCs and state institutions in the cocoa sector. There are furthermore also indirect financial benefits from certification such as improved food security and access to credit and inputs, increased yields, and marketing guarantees, which offer greater benefits than the direct financial benefit of premium price payments (Dompreh et el., 2021; Fenger et al. 2017).

Currently, most farmers are certified only because externally funded projects assist them in maintaining their certification standards (Gockowski et al., 2013; Fenger et al., 2017). This poses a huge risk to the sustainability of these schemes, as such structures might not always be available. Fenger et al. (2017) and Paschall and Seville (2012) therefore discuss the need for farmer-led independent institutions to take up the role of ensuring the sustainability of the environmental, social, and educational benefits currently accrued through certification schemes.

One major challenge discussed in the certification literature relates to farmers selling their certified produce outside the certification value chain (Paschall & Seville, 2012; Fenger et al., 2017). Farmers' reasons for doing this include social relations with purchasing clerks (PCs) of other LBCs, need for cash at a time when the PC for the certification organization has no money to pay for the produce or when they know their produce would be used to settle previous loan commitments (Fenger et al., 2017). In other instances, farmers have been given advanced loans by PCs for other LBCs and use the produce to settle such loans (Fenger et al., 2017). Selling certified produce outside the value chain weakens the certification process as certification institutions need to meet an output quota to be financially sustainable, especially after the initial external financial support is exhausted (Fenger et al., 2017).

Other challenges relate to reported reductions in yields from some certified shaded cocoa systems. For instance, Gockowski et al. (2013) discuss a yield shortage of 274 kg/ha between a Rainforest Alliance certified shaded cocoa system and an intensive full sun system. It is however too hasty to conclude that cocoa agroforestry systems affect farmer livelihoods negatively based on this reported reduction in yields alone as other important factors such as the value of agroforestry products for domestic consumption and associated household food security improvements (Cerda et al., 2014) must be considered. There could also be further benefits from cocoa agroforestry systems if payment for environmental services, which have the prospect to moderate any reductions in yields, materialize (Waldron et al., 2015). For example, the Rainforest Alliance system can provide higher incomes or incomes closer to what the full sun system gives farmers when premiums paid to farmers are added. Also, as already discussed for most cocoa agroforestry systems, farmers are likely to spend less on inputs and agrochemicals in managing Rainforest Alliance farms compared to the high inputs required to manage full sun productions systems. This reduced cost could mean high productive efficiency in these Rainforest Alliance cocoa farms compared to the high input full sun farms.

Service Delivery Models

Many large buyers in the cocoa value chain are now involved in service delivery models (SDM) as part of their sustainability initiatives. Under such models, farmers are provided with bundled services such as training, extension advice, access to inputs and financial support, and physical infrastructure that aim to improve cocoa farmers' cultivation practices, yields, household incomes, sustainability awareness, and well-being (IDH & New Foresight, 2016). SDMs thereby not only support existing governance structures but improve farmers' performance in relation to company sustainability objectives. An example of such a model in Ghana is the ECOM sustainable management services (SMS) (IDH & New Foresight, 2016). SMS supports cocoa farming communities through physical infrastructure such as resource centers, health posts, water, and sanitation facilities in addition to services such as training in fertilizer and crop protection and farmer organization (IDH & New Foresight, 2016). This service delivery mechanism is structured and delivered through a number of Farmer Development Centers (FDCs) in which lead farmers from the communities are trained in good agricultural, environmental, and business practices by personnel employed by SMS so that they can work with farmers on demonstration farms to transfer the knowledge gained (IDH & New Foresight, 2016). Farmers in return are required to supply their cocoa to ECOM to improve the company's sustainability and produce traceability goals. There are also examples of SDMs being carried out to show corporate social responsibility without the buying company intending to purchase cocoa from the farmers.

The major challenge related to ECOM SMS is how to sustain the services in the future as SMS currently bears most of the implementation cost, with farmers only paying for some of the services provided, such as sustaining already established community nurseries. This means the FDCs might collapse if SMS withdraws (IDH & New Foresight, 2016). SDMs are a relatively new approach that is still being trialed so there are several unknowns relating to cost-effectiveness, scalability, and financial self-sustainability. Additionally, SDMs may cause the same problems as certification schemes that lead to farmers focusing on a single cash crop, resulting in less diversified land use and more risky business for farmers if they are not supported by crop insurance schemes (Odijie, 2018).

ICT and Advisory Services

Among smallholder farmers in developing countries the widespread use of mobile phones enables fast transfer of knowledge and business (Baumüller, 2017, 2018). Information and service delivery within the cocoa sector continues to benefit from such advancements. In Ghana, the presence of CocoaLink implemented by Farmerline, Hershey, World Cocoa Foundation, and COCOBOD, the Olam Farmer Information System (OFIS), and sustainable management services (SMS) by ECOM are a few examples of initiatives that rely on the rapid advancement and penetration of ICT in cocoa cultivation areas to deliver both advisory services and targeted development initiatives in cocoa communities. These services have been used to compensate for the lack of access to formal agricultural knowledge systems (Huyer, 2016), the main rationale being that by making more knowledge and information available to cocoa farmers they can significantly improve their cultivation systems as well as yields.

CocoaLink is an agricultural extension tool, which relies on the growing mobile technology presence in rural Ghana to provide cocoa farmers with important farming, social, and marketing information in a timely manner (Aidoo, 2014). This service employs a two-way communication approach (Liu & Garloch, 2012) and provides a range of services including reinforcement messages, training locals as community facilitators, weekly education sessions, and national extension agent support (Aidoo, 2014). Within CocoaLink, farmers can request agricultural information and advice through SMS and a mobile application. Further, weekly push messages are sent by the implementing organization World Education Inc. in collaboration with local partners in Accra to all registered cocoa farmers (Liu & Garloch, 2012). This service is an important outreach program, which has the potential to improve both the quality of and farmers' access to extension services in the cocoa sector (Bell et al., 2013).

The Olam Farmer Information System (OFIS), which collects farmer and farm data through surveys to provide targeted and personalized agricultural advice and long-term plans to farmers, is another example of an ICT-based service that is being implemented in over 30 countries, including Ghana (FAO & ITU, 2019; Olam International Limited, 2021). Through SMS, farmers receive information on pricing, weather forecasts, and agricultural advice. The platform service aims to allow farmers to communicate directly with field staff and features a business management functionality for organizational management and record keeping and a digital payments system, which allows them to access financial services (Olam International Limited, 2017a; FAO & ITU, 2019). An aspect of the system includes geo-tagging of farms (FAO &

ITU, 2019) and bag coding (Olam International Limited, 2017b), which makes end-to-end product traceability possible.

The impacts of these ICT-led advisory services have not been extensively studied in Ghana, but existing studies on these developments elsewhere are optimistic concerning their potential for improving agricultural advisory services (Baumüller, 2018). ICT-led models can improve farmers' access to knowledge, credit services, input supply channels, and time-sensitive information because such models, unlike traditional agricultural advisory channels, do not require physical contact with extension and service agents (Kos & Kloppenburg, 2019). ICT-led models have the additional advantage of appealing to youth. However, there are some significant challenges and disadvantages of primarily delivering agricultural advisory services mainly through such fast-paced ICT innovative solutions. Most ICT and app-based advisory services rely on initial investments in mobile technology. This presents some accessibility and scalability challenges to farmers and service providers mainly due to high poverty levels in some cocoa households and the poor network connectivity characteristic of most cocoa zones in Ghana. There are also general concerns regarding ownership, access, and use of farmers information, especially by third-party interests, new burdens on farmers to collect data, and companies benefiting financially from farmers' data at their expense (Kos & Kloppenburg, 2019).

3.4 Conclusion: Innovation and the Future of Cocoa Production

This chapter has shown that for innovations to lead to sustainable cocoa cultivation they must not only contribute to the ability to mitigate and adapt to climate change and maximize yields. They must also address multiple broader challenges. Cocoa production continues to contribute the majority of income for the about 550,000 cocoa farming households in the country (Ghana Statistical Service, 2019) and has played a significant role toward poverty alleviation in the forest regions of Ghana (Stanturf et al., 2011). Yet, currently the average age of cocoa farmers in Ghana is above 50 years (Asamoah et al., 2015). This is partly explained by the next generation of cocoa farmers being pushed to pursue other career options because of a growing shortage and fragmentation of land caused by population increases, the lack of new frontiers for expansion, customary land tenure (Kidido et al. 2017), and decades of inequitable cocoa land sharing and/or sharecropping arrangements (Kansanga et al., 2018). When coupled with poor access to extension/training services, and poorly structured farmer-based organizations cocoa farming has become increasingly unattractive (Stanturf et al., 2011; UNDP, 2012; Djokoto et al., 2016).

With the current focus on issues related to the changing climate, a primary international concern has been how cocoa farmers can adapt to climate change and how to create a more environmentally sustainable cocoa farming system. However, the challenges to cocoa farming are not only environmental, but also social. An aging cocoa farmer population poses numerous challenges to the adoption of innovations, improved practices and technologies (Barrientos et al., 2008; Djokoto et al., 2016) as such farmers are more likely to be conservative compared to young cocoa farmers who are more likely to be innovative. Youth involvement is therefore paramount to creating sustainable cocoa production. Youths, however, want social mobility and do not wish to be engaged in farming as laborers or caretakers, but rather as farmers with clear rights to the land—and possibly with a non-farm primary occupation and farming as a secondary activity (Anyidoho et al., 2012: 29). As highlighted by Anyidoho et al. (2012: 30): "Policies should recognize and seek to resolve this tension, rather than seeking to constrain young people's attempts at physical and social mobility".

New sustainable innovations and practices spanning agricultural advisory/training services, social and community infrastructure, and environmental services that are currently being introduced by non-state actors in the cocoa value chain, especially large trading and chocolate manufacturing companies, show some potential in this regard. These companies, however, are largely driven by commercial interests and their desire to demonstrate their sustainability profile (Olwig, 2021). Furthermore, while companies can address certain challenges because of their access to resources and technology that may, for example, improve the attractiveness of cocoa farming to youth, other challenges, such as land rights and land usage, can only be overcome through close collaboration with the government. This analysis thus calls for a more holistic approach to the study and implementation of climate-induced innovation in the context of climate change mitigation as well as climate change adaptation strategies.

Funding The work was supported by Danida [Ministry of Foreign Affairs of Denmark] through "Climate Smart Cocoa Systems for Ghana, CLIMCOCOA", DFC project no: 16-P02-GHA.

References

Abdulai, I., Vaast, P., Hoffmann, M. P., Asare, R., Jassogne, L., Van Asten, P., Rötter, R. P., & Graefe, S. (2018). Cocoa agroforestry is less resilient to sub-optimal and extreme climate than cocoa in full sun. *Global Change Biology*, 24(1), 273–286. https://doi.org/10.1111/gcb.13885.

Abdulai, I., Hoffmann, M. P., Jassogne, L., Asare, R., Graefe, S., Tao, H.-H., et al. (2020). Variations in yield gaps of smallholder cocoa systems and the main determining factors along a climate gradient in Ghana. *Agricultural Systems*, 181, 102812. https://doi.org/10.1016/j.agsy.2020.102812.

Aidoo, R. (2014). Final Evaluation Report CocoaLink Ghana. Available online at: https://cocoasoils.org/wp-content/uploads/2019/02/CocoaLink-_End line-evaluation_distribution2.pdf (Accessed 18 November 2019).

Ali, E. B., Awuni, J. A., & Danso-Abbeam, G. (2018). Determinants of fertilizer adoption among smallholder cocoa farmers in the Western Region of Ghana. *Cogent Food & Agriculture*, 4(1), 1538589. https://doi.org/10.1080/23311932.2018.1538589.

Alliance for a Green Revolution in Africa [AGRA]. (2014). *Africa Agriculture Status Report 2014: Climate change and smallholder agriculture in sub-Saharan Africa*. Nairobi: AGRA.

Amankwaah, B. A., Asomaning, G., Atuguba, R. A., Ayifah, E., Brudney, A., Citro, B., Ryerson, C., Sarkwah, S. K., & Tarzikhan, A. (2021). *COCOBOD's Unrealised potential: Promoting human rights, welfare, and the environment in Ghana's cocoa-growing communities*. Northwestern Pritzker School of Law Center for International Human Rights, University of Ghana School of Law, Corporate Accountability Lab & SEND Ghana.

Amanor, K.S. (1996). *Managing trees in the farming system: The perspective of farmers*. Ghana Forestry Department, Forest Farming Series. Kumasi, Ghana: Forestry Department Planning Branch.

Amlalo, D., & Oppong-Boadi, K. (2015). *Ghana's Third National Communication Report to the UNFCCC*. Accra: EPA & MESTI. Available online at: unfccc.int/resource/docs/natc/ghanc3.pdf (Accessed 6 September 2016).

Aneani, F., & Padi, F. (2017). Baseline farmer survey of smallholder cocoa farming systems in Ghana. *Sustainable Agriculture Research*, 6(1), 13–23. https://doi.org/10.5539/sar.v6n1p13.

Aneani, F., Anchirinah, V. M., Asamoah, M. & Owusu-Ansah, F. (2011). Analysis of economic efficiency in cocoa production in Ghana. *African Journal of Food, Agriculture, Nutrition and Development*, 11(1), 4507–4526.

Anyidoho, N.A., Leavy, J., & Asenso-Okyere, K. (2012). Perceptions and aspirations: A case study of young people in Ghana's cocoa sector. *IDS Bulletin*, 43(6), 20–32.

Asamoah, M., Aneani, F., Ofori, S., & Branor, P. F. (2015). Analysis of farmers adoption behaviour of CRIG recommended technologies as a package: The case of some self help cocoa farmer associations in the Eastern Region of Ghana. *Agricultural Sciences*, 6, 601–608. https://doi.org/10.4236/as.2015.66059.

Asare, R. (2005). *Cocoa agroforests in West Africa: A look at activities on preferred trees in the farming systems*. Copenhagen: Forest & Landscape Denmark (FLD).

Asare R (2006) *Learning about neighbour trees in cocoa growing systems- a manual for farmer trainers*. Forest & Landscape Development and Environment Series no. 4-2006.

Asare, R. (2019). The nexus between cocoa production and deforestation. *Grain de Sel*, 78, 26–27.

Asare, R., Afari-sefa, V., Gyamfi, I., Okafor, C., & Mva, J. M. (2010). *Cocoa seed multiplication: an assessment of seed gardens in Cameroon, Ghana and Nigeria*. The Sustainable Tree Crops Program (STCP) Working Paper Series Issue 11 (Version August 2010). Acccra: International Institute of Tropical Agriculture.

Asare, R., Afari-Sefa, V., & Muilerman, S. (2016). Access to improved hybrid seeds in Ghana: Implications for establishment and rehabilitation of cocoa farms. *Experimental Agriculture*, 54(2), 273–285. https://doi.org/10.1017/S0014479716000247.

Asare, R., Afari-Sefa, V., Osei-Owusu, Y. & Pabi, O. (2014). Cocoa agroforestry for increasing forest connectivity in a fragmented landscape in Ghana. *Agroforestry Systems*, 88, 1143–1156. https://doi.org/10.1007/s10457-014-9688-3.

Asare, R., Afari-Sefa, V., Muilerman, S., & Anim-Kwapong, G. J. (2018). Good agronomic practices in cocoa cultivation: Rehabilitating cocoa farms. In: P. Umaharan (Ed.), *Achieving sustainable cultivation of cocoa*. Cambridge: Burleigh Dodds Science Publishing. https://doi.org/10.19103/AS.2017.0021.12.

Bandanaa, J., Egyir, I. S., & Asante, I. (2016). Cocoa farming households in Ghana consider organic practices as climate smart and livelihoods enhancer. *Agriculture & Food Security*, 5(1), 29. https://doi.org/10.1186/s40066-016-0077-1.

Barima, Y. S. S., Kouakou, A. T. M., Bamba, I., Sangne, Y. C., Godron, M., Andrieu, J., & Bogaert, J. (2016). Cocoa crops are destroying the forest reserves of the classified forest of Haut-Sassandra (Ivory Coast). *Global Ecology and Conservation*, 8, 85–98. https://doi.org/10.1016/j.gecco.2016.08.009.

Barrientos, S., Asenso-Okyere, K., Asuming-Brempong, S., Sarpong, D., Anyidoho, N., Kaplinsky, R., & Leavy, S. (2008). *Mapping sustainable production in Ghanaian cocoa*. Report to Cadbury Schweppes plc.

Baumüller, H. (2017). Towards smart farming? Mobile technology trends and their potential for developing country agriculture. In: K. E. Skouby, I. Williams, & A. Gyamfi (Eds.), *Handbook for ICT in developing countries: 5G perspectives* (pp. 191–201). Delft: River Publishers.

Baumüller, H. (2018). The little we know: An exploratory literature review on the utility of mobile phone-enabled services for smallholder farmers. *Journal of International Development*, 30(1), 134–154. https://doi.org/10.1002/jid.3314.

Bell, M., Bohn, A., Teiken, C., Madden, N., Peach-fine, E., Schweiger, J., & Shuck, J. (2013). *Rapid assessment of the ICT for agriculture extension landscape in Ghana*. USAID.

Bunn, C., Läderach, P., Quaye, A., Muilerman, S., Noponen, M. R. A. & Lundy, M. (2019). Recommendation domains to scale out climate change adaptation in cocoa production in Ghana. *Climate Services*, 16, 100123. https://doi.org/10.1016/j.cliser.2019.100123.

Cerda, R., Deheuvels, O., Calvache, D., Niehaus, L., Saenz, Y., Kent, J., Vilchez, S., Villota, A., Martinez, C., & Somarriba, E. (2014). Contribution of cocoa agroforestry systems to family income and domestic consumption: Looking toward intensification. *Agroforestry Systems*, 88(6), 957–981. https://doi.org/10.1007/s10457-014-9691-8.

Clough, Y., Faust, H., & Tscharntke, T. (2009). Cacao boom and bust: sustainability of agroforests and opportunities for biodiversity conservation. *Conservation Letters*, 2(5), 197–205. https://doi.org/10.1111/j.1755-263x.2009.00072.x.

Cobbina, J. (2014). *Technical efficiency of cocoa production in Ghana: A case study of Upper Denkyira East Municipality*. Master of Philosophy Thesis, Kwame Nkrumah University of Science and Technology.

COCOBOD. (2021). *Regional cocoa purchases*. Available online at: https://cocobod.gh/cocoa-purchases (Accessed 8 August 2021).

Dagar, J. C., & Tewari, V. P. (2017). Chapter 2: Evolution of agroforestry as a modern science. In: J. C. Dagar & V. P. Tewari (Eds.), *Agroforestry: Anecdotal to modern science* (pp. 13–90). Singapore: Springer Nature Singapore Pte Ltd.

Daghela Bisseleua, H. B., Fotio, D., Missoup, A. D., & Vidal, S. (2013). Shade tree diversity, cocoa pest damage, yield compensating inputs and farmers' net returns in West Africa. *PLoS ONE*, 8(3), e56115. https://doi.org/10.1371/journal.pone.0056115.

Djokoto, J. G., Owusu, V., & Awunyo-Vitor, D. (2016). Adoption of organic agriculture: Evidence from cocoa farming in Ghana. *Cogent Food & Agriculture*, 2(1), 1242181. https://doi.org/10.1080/23311932.2016.1242181.

Dompreh, E. B., Asare, R., & Gasparatos, A. (2021). Sustainable but hungry? Food security outcomes of certification for cocoa and oil palm smallholders in Ghana. *Environmental Research Letters*, 16 (2021), 055001. https://doi.org/10.1088/1748-9326/abdf88.

Dormon, E. N. A., Van Huis, A., Leeuwis, C., Obeng-Ofori, D., & Sakyi-Dawson, O. (2004). Causes of low productivity of cocoa in Ghana: Farmers' perspectives and insights from research and the socio-political establishment. *NJAS-Wageningen Journal of life Science*, 52(3–4), 237–259. https://doi.org/10.1016/S1573-5214(04)80016-2.

Fahmid, I. M., Harun, H., Fahmid, M. M., Saadah, & Busthanul, N. (2018). Competitiveness, production, and productivity of cocoa in Indonesia. *IOP Conference Series: Earth and Environmental Science*, 157(012067). https://doi.org/10.1088/1755-1315/157/1/012067.

FAO. (2018). *FAO's work on agricultural innovation: Sowing the seeds of transformation to achieve the SDGs*. FAO Brochure, CA2460EN/1/11.18. Available online at: http://www.fao.org/3/CA2460EN/ca2460en.pdf (Accessed 11 March 2020).

FAO & ITU. (2019). *E-Agriculture in action: Big data for agriculture*. Bangkok: Food and Agriculture Organization and the International Telecommunication Union.

FAOSTAT. (2020). Available at http://www.fao.org/faostat/en/#data/QCL.

Fenger, N., Bosselmann, A. S., Asare, R., & Neergaard, A. (2017). The impact of certification on the natural and financial capitals of Ghanaian cocoa farmers. *Agroecology and Sustainable Food Systems*, 41(2), 143–166. https://doi.org/10.1080/21683565.2016.1258606.

Franzen, M., & Borgerhoff Mulder, M. (2007). Ecological, economic and social perspectives on cocoa production worldwide. *Biodiversity Conservation*, 16, 3835–3849. https://doi.org/10.1007/s10531-007-9183-5.

Ghana Statistical Service. (2019). *Ghana Living Standards Survey Round 7 (GLSS 7) Main report*. Accra: Ghana Statistical Service.

Glin, L. C., Oosterveer, P., & Mol, A. P. (2015). Governing the organic cocoa network from Ghana: Towards hybrid governance arrangements? *Journal of Agrarian Change*, 15(1), 43–64. https://doi.org/10.1111/joac.12059.

Gockowski, J., & Sonwa, D. (2011). Cocoa intensification scenarios and their predicted impact on CO_2 emissions, biodiversity conservation, and rural livelihoods in the Guinea rain forest of West Africa. *Environmental Management*, 48(2), 307–321. https://doi.org/10.1007/s00267-010-9602-3.

Gockowski, J., Afari-Sefa, V., Sarpong, D. B., Osei-Asare, Y. B., & Agyeman, N. F. (2013). Improving the productivity and income of Ghanaian cocoa farmers while maintaining environmental services: What role for certification? *International Journal of Agricultural Sustainability*, 114, 331–346. https://doi.org/10.1080/14735903.2013.772714.

Gockowski, J., Robiglio, V., Muilerman, S., & Agyeman, N. F. (2011). *Agricultural intensification as a strategy for climate mitigation in Ghana: An evaluative study of the COCOBOD High Tech Program, rural incomes and forest resources in the Bia (Juaboso) District of Ghana*. A Sustainable Tree Crops Program Report, International Institute of Tropical Agriculture.

Gockowski, J., Tchatat, M., Dondjang, J. P., Hietet, G., & Fouda, T. (2010). An empirical analysis of the biodiversity and economic returns to cocoa agroforests in Southern Cameroon. *Journal of Sustainable Forestry*, 29(6–8), 638–670. https://doi.org/10.1080/10549811003739486.

Graefe, S., Meyer-Sand, L. F., Chauvette, K., Abdulai, I., Jassogne, L., Vaast, P., & Asare, R. (2017). Evaluating farmers' knowledge of shade trees in different cocoa agro-ecological zones in Ghana. *Human Ecology*, 45(3), 321–332. https://doi.org/10.1007/s10745-017-9899-0.

Hutchins, A., Tamargo, A., Bailey, Y., & Kim, Y. (2015) *Assessment of climate change impacts on cocoa production and approaches to adaptation and mitigation: A contextual view of Ghana and Costa Rica* (p. 16). International Development Studies.

Huyer, S. (2016). Closing the gender gap in agriculture. *Gender, Technology and Development*, 20(2), 105–116. https://doi.org/10.1177/0971852416643872.

IDH, & New Foresight. (2016). *SDM: ECOM/SMS Ghana—Service delivery model assessment*. Available online at: https://www.idhsustainabletrade.com/uploaded/2016/10/SDM-full-case-report-ECOM-Ghana.pdf (Accessed 14 October 2019).

Ingram, V., van Rijn, F., Waarts, Y., & Gilhuis, H. (2018). The impacts of cocoa sustainability initiatives in West Africa. *Sustainability (Switzerland)*, 10(11), 4249. https://doi.org/10.3390/su10114249.

International Federation of Organic Agriculture Movements [IFOAM]. (2010). *Definition of organic agriculture*. Available online at: https://www.ifoam.bio/en/organic-landmarks/definition-organic-agriculture (Accessed 20 October 2017).

IPCC. (2014). *Climate Change 2014: Impacts, adaptation, and vulnerability. Part A: Global and sectoral aspects. Contribution of Working Group II to the Fifth Assessment Report of the Intergovernmental Panel on Climate Change* [Field, C. B., V. R. Barros, D. J. Dokken, K. J. Mach, M. D. Mastrandrea, T.E. Bilir, M. Chatterjee, K.L. Ebi, Y.O. Estrada, R.C. Genova, B. Girma,

E. S. Kissel, A. N. Levy, S. MacCracken, P. R. Mastrandrea, & L. L. White (Eds.)]. Cambridge and New York: Cambridge University Press, 1132 pp.

Kansanga, M., Andersen, P., Atuoye, K., & Mason-Renton, S. (2018). Contested commons: Agricultural modernization, tenure ambiguities and intra-familial land grabbing in Ghana. *Land Use Policy*, 75, 215–224. https://doi.org/10.1016/j.landusepol.2018.03.047.

Kidido, J. K., Bugri, J. T., & Kasanga, R., K. (2017). Dynamics of youth access to agricultural land under the customary tenure regime in the Techiman traditional area of Ghana. *Land Use Policy*, 60, 254–266. https://doi.org/10.1016/j.landusepol.2016.10.040.

Kolavalli, S., & Vigneri, M. (2011). Cocoa in Ghana: Shaping the success of an economy. In: P. Chuhan-Pole & M. Angwafo (Eds.), *Yes, Africa can: Success stories from a dynamic continent* (pp. 201–217). Washington, DC: World Bank Publication.

Kolavalli, S., & Vigneri, M. (2017). *The cocoa coast: The board-managed cocoa sector in Ghana*. Washington, DC: International Food Policy Research Institute (IFPRI). https://doi.org/10.2499/9780896292680.

Kos, D., & Kloppenburg, S. (2019). Digital technologies, hyper-transparency and smallholder farmer inclusion in global value chains. *Current Opinion in Environmental Sustainability*, 41, 56–63. https://doi.org/10.1016/j.cosust.2019.10.011.

Kroeger, A., Bakhtary, H., Haupt, F., & Streck, C. (2017a). *Eliminating deforestation from the cocoa supply chain*. Washington, DC: The World Bank.

Kroeger, A., Koenig, S., Thomson, A., & Streck, C. (2017b). *Forest- and climate-smart cocoa in Côte d'Ivoire and Ghana, aligning stakeholders to support smallholders in deforestation-free cocoa*. Washington, DC: World Bank.

Liu, A. T., & Garloch, A. C. (2012). *COCOALINK (ICT and AG Profile)*. Available online at: https://www.marketlinks.org/sites/marketlinks.org/files/resource/files/CocoaLinkprofile.pdf (Accessed 14 October 2019).

Läderach, P., Martinez-Valle, A., Schroth, G., & Castro, N. (2013). Predicting the future climatic suitability for cocoa farming of the world's leading producer countries, Ghana and Côte d'Ivoire. *Climatic Change*, 119(3–4), 841–854. https://doi.org/10.1007/s10584-013-0774-8.

McKinley, J., Nalley, L. L., Asare, R. A., Dixon, B. L., Popp, J. S., & D'Haese, M. (2016). Managing risk in cocoa production: assessing the potential of climate-smart crop insurance in Ghana. *Journal of International Agricultural Trade and Development*, 10(1), 53–79.

McSweeney, C., New, M., & Lizcano, G. (2010). *UNDP climate change country profiles: Ghana*. https://www.geog.ox.ac.uk/research/climate/projects/undp-cp/UNDP_reports/Ghana/Ghana.lowres.report.pdf (Accessed 10 April 2017).

Meier, C., Sampson, G., Larrea, C., Schlatter, B., Voora, V., Dang, D., Bermudez, S., Wozniak, J., & Willer, H. (2020). *The state of sustainable markets 2020: Statistics and emerging trends*. Geneva: International Trade Centre (ITC).

Meijer, S. S., Catacutan, D., Ajayi, O. C., Sileshi, G. W., & Nieuwenhuis, M. (2015). The role of knowledge, attitudes and perceptions in the uptake of agricultural and agroforestry innovations among smallholder farmers in sub-Saharan Africa. *International Journal of Agricultural Sustainability*, 13(1), 40–54. https://doi.org/10.1080/14735903.2014.912493.

Mondelēz International. (2015). *Cocoa life: Empowering cocoa farmers and communities*. https://www.cocoalife.org/~/media/cocoalife/Files/pdf/Library/Cocoa%20Life%20Progress%20Report (Accessed 1 May 2017).

Muilerman, S., & Vellema, S. (2017). Scaling service delivery in a failed state: Cocoa smallholders, Farmer Field Schools, persistent bureaucrats and institutional work in Côte d'Ivoire. *International Journal of Agricultural Sustainability*, 15(1), 83–98. https://doi.org/10.1080/14735903.2016.1246274.

Munthali, N., Leeuwis, C., van Paassen, A., Lie, R., Asare, R., van Lammeren, R., & Schut, M. (2018). Innovation intermediation in a digital age: Comparing public and private new-ICT platforms for agricultural extension in Ghana. *NJAS-Wageningen Journal of Life Sciences*, 86, 64–76. https://doi.org/10.1016/j.njas.2018.05.001.

Naminse, E. Y., Fosu, M., & Nongyenge, Y. (2011). *The impact of mass spraying programme on cocoa production in Ghana*. Report on Field Survey. University for Development Studies, Ghana.

Neufeldt, H., Wilkes, A., Zomer, R. J., Xu, J., Nang'ole, E., Munster, C., & Place, F. (2009). *Trees on farms: Tackling the triple challenges of mitigation, adaptation and food security*. World Agroforestry Centre Policy Brief 07. Nairobi: World Agroforestry Centre.

Nunoo, I., & Owusu, V. (2017). Comparative analysis on financial viability of cocoa agroforestry systems in Ghana. *Environment, Development and Sustainability*, 19(1), 83–98. https://doi.org/10.1007/s10668-015-9733-z.

Nunoo, I., Obiri, B. D., & Frimpong, B. N. (2015). *From deforestation to afforestation: Evidence from cocoa agroforestry systems*. In: XIV World Forestry Congress, Durban, South Africa (pp. 7–11).

Obiri, B. D., Bright, G. A., McDonald, M. A., Anglaaere, L. C., & Cobbina, J. (2007). Financial analysis of shaded cocoa in Ghana. *Agroforestry Systems*, 71(2), 139–149. https://doi.org/10.1007/s10457-007-9058-5.

Odijie, M. E. (2018). Sustainability winners and losers in business-biased cocoa sustainability programmes in West Africa. *International Journal of Agricultural Sustainability*, 16(2), 214–227. https://doi.org/10.1080/14735903.2018.1445408.

Olam International Limited. (2017a). *Olam Farmer Information System (OFIS)—Revolutionary technology solution for collecting and applying farmgate level data*. Available online at: https://www.olamgroup.com/content/dam/olamgroup/files/uploads/2017a/07/New-OFIS-Brochure-1.pdf (Accessed 14 October 2019).

Olam International Limited. (2017b). *Olam Farmer Information System (OFIS)—Revolutionary technology solution for gathering and utilising farm-gate level data*. Available online at: http://olamgroup.com/sustainability/ofis/ (Accessed 14 October 2019).

Olam International Limited. (2021). *Olam Farmer Information System: Ending the isolation of rural farming and boosting traceability*. Available online at: https://www.olamgroup.com/sustainability/innovation-technology/farmgate/olam-farmer-information-system.html (Accessed 11 August 2021).

Olwig, M. F. (2012). Multi-sited resilience: The mutual construction of "local" and "global" understandings and practices of adaptation and innovation. *Applied Geography*, 33, 112–118. https://doi.org/10.1016/j.apgeog.2011.10.007.

Olwig, M. F. (2021) Sustainability superheroes? For-profit narratives of 'doing good' in the era of the SDGs. *World Development*, 142. https://doi.org/10.1016/j.worlddev.2021.105427.

Ongolo, S., Kouassi, S. K., Chérif, S., & Giessen, L. (2018). The tragedy of forestland sustainability in postcolonial Africa: Land development, Cocoa, and politics in Côte d'Ivoire. *Sustainability (Switzerland)*, 10(12), 1–17. https://doi.org/10.3390/su10124611.

Owusu, K., & Waylen, P. R. (2009). Trends in spatio-temporal rainfall variability in Ghana (1951–2000). *Weather*, 64, 115–120.

Padi, F. K., Adu-Gyamfi, P., Akpertey, A., Arthur, A., & Ofori, A. (2013). Differential response of cocoa (Theobroma cacao) families to field establishment stress. *Plant Breeding*, 132(2), 229–236. https://doi.org/10.1111/pbr.12039.

Paschall, M., & Seville, D. (2012). *Certified Cocoa: scaling up farmer participation in West Africa*. New Business Models for Sustainable Trading Relationships Case Study Series. London: IIED. Available online at: http://pubs.iied.org/16034IIED.html.

Proven Ag Solutions. (2014). *Review of the existing tree tenure policies and legislations and their implications for the cocoa sector in Ghana*. Final Report to Ghana COCOBOD and UNDP Ghana, Environmental Sustainability and Policy for Cocoa Production in Ghana Project. Available online at: http://www.gh.undp.org/content/dam/ghana/docs/Doc/Susdev/FINAL%20REPORT%20-%20TREE%20TENURE%20REVIEW.pdf (Accessed 8 August 2019).

Reganold, J. P., & Wachter, J. M. (2016). Organic agriculture in the twenty-first century. *Nature Plants*, 2(2), 15221. https://doi.org/10.1038/nplants.2015.221.

Rodima-Taylor, D., Olwig, M. F., & Chhetri, N. (2012). Adaptation as innovation, innovation as adaptation: An institutional approach to climate change. *Applied Geography*, 33, 107–111. https://doi.org/10.1016/j.apgeog.2011.10.011.

Rodríguez-Fonseca, B., Janicot, S., Mohino, E., Losada, T., Bader, J., Caminade, C., Chauvin, F., Fontaine, B., García-Serrano, J., Gervois, S., Joly, M., Polo, I., Ruti, P., Rouco, P., & Voldoire, A. (2011). Interannual and decadal SST-forced responses of the West African monsoon. *Atmospheric Science Letters*, 12, 67–74. https://doi.org/10.1002/asl.308.

Roth, M., Antwi, Y., & O'Sullivan, R. (2017). *Land and natural resource governance and tenure for enabling sustainable cocoa cultivation in Ghana*. Washington, DC: USAID Tenure and Global Climate Change Program.

Ruf, F. O. (2011). The myth of complex cocoa agroforests: The case of Ghana. *Human Ecology*, 39(3), 373–388. https://doi.org/10.1007/s10745-011-9392-0.

Ruf, F., & Schroth, G. (2004). Chocolate forests and monocultures: a historical review of cocoa growing and its conflicting role in tropical deforestation and forest conservation. In: G. Schroth, G. A. B. da Fonseca, C. A. Harvey, C. Gascon, H. L. Vasconcelos, & A.-M. N. Izac (Eds.), *Agroforestry and biodiversity conservation in tropical landscapes* (pp. 107–134). Washington, DC: Island Press.

Sadhu, S., Kysia, K., Onyango, L., Zinnes, C. F., Lord, S., Monnard, A., & Arellano, I. R. (2020). *Assessing progress in reducing child labor in cocoa production in cocoa growing areas of Côte d'Ivoire and Ghana*. NORC, University of Chicago.

Scott, G., Donovan, J., & Higuchi, A. (2016). Costs, quality, and competition in the cocoa value chain in Peru: An exploratory assessment. *Custos e @gronegócio on line*, 11(4), 324–358.

Stanturf, J. A., Warren, M. L., Charnley Jr, S., Polasky, S. C., Goodrick, S. L., Armah, F., & Nyako, Y. A. (2011). *Ghana climate change vulnerability and adaptation assessment*. Washington, DC: United States Agency for International Development.

Thorlakson, T., & Neufeldt, H. (2012). Reducing subsistence farmers' vulnerability to climate change: Evaluating the potential contributions of agroforestry in western Kenya. *Agriculture & Food Security*, 1 (15). https://doi.org/10.1186/2048-7010-1-15.

Uribe-Leitz, E., & Ruf, F. (2019). Cocoa certification in West Africa: The need for change. In: M. Schmidt, D. Giovannucci, D. Palekhov, & B. Hansmann (Eds.), *Sustainable global value chains* (pp. 435–461). Cham: Springer.

UNDP. (2012). *Environmental sustainability and policy for cocoa production in Ghana*. United Nations Development Programme Project Document. Available online at: http://www.undp.org/content/dam/ghana/docs/Doc/Partner/UNDP_GH_SUSDEV_Environmental%20sustainability%20and%20cocoa%20project.pdf (Accessed 8 June 2016).

Vaast, P., & Somarriba, E. (2014). Trade-offs between crop intensification and ecosystem services: The role of agroforestry in cocoa cultivation. *Agroforestry Systems,* 88(6), 947–956. https://doi.org/10.1007/s10457-014-9762-x

Voora, V., Bermúdez, S., & Larrea, C. (2019). Global Market Report: Cocoa. *Sustainable Commodities Marketplace Series 2019*. Manitoba, Canada: The International Institute for Sustainable Development.

Waldron, A., Justicia, R., & Smith, L. E. (2015). Making biodiversity-friendly cocoa pay: Combining yield, certification, and REDD for shade management. *Ecological Applications*, 25(2), 361–372. https://doi.org/10.1890/13-0313.1.

Wisner, B., Blaikie, P., Cannon, T., & Davis, I. (2004). *At risk: Natural hazards, people's vulnerability, and disasters*. London: Routledge.

Witteveen, L., Lie, R., Goris, M., & Ingram, V. (2017). Design and development of a digital farmer field school. Experiences with a digital learning environment for cocoa production and certification in Sierra Leone. *Telematics and Informatics*, 34(8), 1673–1684. https://doi.org/10.1016/j.tele.2017.07.013.

World Cocoa Foundation. (2014). *Cocoa market update*. Available online at: http://www.worldcocoafoundation.org/wp-content/uploads/Cocoa-Market-Update-as-of-4-1-2014.pdf (Accessed 19 May 2017).

CHAPTER 4

Climate Smart Agriculture: Mitigation and Adaptation Strategies at the Global Scale

Hossein Azadi, Narges Siamian, Stefan Burkart, Saghi Movahhed Moghaddam, Imaneh Goli, Thomas Dogot, Philippe Lebailly, Dereje Teklemariam, Astrida Miceikienė, and Steven Van Passel

Abstract To address adaptation and mitigation strategies for climate change, researchers in the agricultural field have extended numerous technologies and practices known as climate-smart agriculture (CSA). The CSA has led to an important debate on sustainable development in the agriculture system and climate among the scientific and civil society. However, one of the main challenges is incorporating the effects

H. Azadi (✉) · T. Dogot · P. Lebailly
Department of Economics and Rural Development, Gembloux Agro-Bio Tech, University of Liège, Gembloux, Belgium
e-mail: hossein.azadi@uliege.be

T. Dogot
e-mail: thomas.dogot@uliege.be

P. Lebailly
e-mail: philippe.burny@uliege.be

M. Coromaldi and S. Auci (eds.), *Climate-Induced Innovation*,
https://doi.org/10.1007/978-3-031-01330-0_4

of climate change into agricultural development planning. For effective adaptation, the set of technologies that the CSA concept comprises requires measures of policies to decrease vulnerability and improve the capacity of producers, especially smallholders. Therefore, the goal of this chapter is to expand and formalize the CSA conceptual framework by relying on the theory and concepts of global adaptation and mitigation strategies. Overall, the chapter provides some evidence of good practices

H. Azadi
Ghent, Belgium

N. Siamian
Faculty of Natural Resources and Environment, Science and Research Branch, Department of Environmental Science, Islamic Azad University, Tehran, Iran
e-mail: narges.siamian@srbiau.ac.ir

S. Burkart
Tropical Forages Program, The Alliance of Bioversity International and the International Center for Tropical Agriculture (CIAT), Cali, Colombia
e-mail: S.Burkart@CGIAR.ORG

S. M. Moghaddam
Faculty of Environmental Sciences, Czech University of Life Sciences Prague, Prague, Czech Republic
e-mail: movahhed_moghaddam@fzp.czu.cz

I. Goli
Department of Economics, Agricultural Extension and Education, Tehran Science and Research Branch, Islamic Azad University, Tehran, Iran
e-mail: imaneh.goli@srbiau.ac.ir

D. Teklemariam
Department of Management, Debre Berhan University, Debre Berhan, Ethiopia
e-mail: dereje.t@ecsu.edu.et

A. Miceikienė
Agriculture Academy, Vytautas Magnus University, Kaunas distr, Lithuania
e-mail: astrida.miceikiene@vdu.lt

S. Van Passel
Department of Engineering Management, University of Antwerp, Antwerp, Belgium
e-mail: Steven.VanPassel@uantwerpen.be

and innovative strategies of upgrading the CSA approach to mitigation and adaptation strategies through development agencies and civil society, research and academia, etc.

Keywords Climate change · Resource management · Food security · Resilience · Sustainability

4.1 Introduction

In recent decades, climate change has been taken as a constant factor affecting the economic conditions of different sectors, in particular the agricultural sector. The agriculture sector and climate change are interrelated in various ways. In other words, climate change makes the agricultural sector vulnerable, and greenhouse gas (GHG) emissions are a significant source of these changes (Chandra et al. 2018). The capacity of the agricultural sector to convert carbon dioxide from the atmosphere through photosynthesis into food and thus compensating for part of the GHG produced, is unique (Boone et al. 2018).

Climate change is changing rapidly and positively and negatively affecting various aspects of agriculture. In other words, the negative effects such as severe drought, hurricanes, and increasing levels of the sea are more threatening and require quick and lasting solutions. However, these solutions should not cause more climate change. The concept of climate smart agriculture (CSA) is considered by experts as one of the answers since it involves climate-resilient technologies and practices, while addressing matters of reducing GHG emissions. Therefore, in the first part of this chapter, the impact of climate change on agriculture, the importance of CSA, and its dimensions will be described.

Effect of Climate Change on Agriculture

The climate change effect on the agricultural sector is often expressed as a consequence of climate extremes on agriculture. In numerous cases, it is considered as a shift in climate variables and its further effects on livestock and agricultural production. Climate change causes changes in ecosystems and leads to natural phenomena, such as an increase in the average atmospheric temperature, a rising sea level, shifts in rainfall patterns, increases in temperature fluctuations, and reductions in the groundwater levels.

In addition, the effect of climate phenomena, e.g., floods and droughts, often cause limited access to food and water, economic instability, and food insecurity. Generally, crop yields rather decrease in the currently warm regions with naturally low precipitation levels. Additionally, conditions become more difficult in areas where the temperature is below the optimal values for the production and growth of plants and crops. Rice and wheat are the crops that may profit more than crops such as corn and sugar cane due to the impact of CO_2 fertilization in high CO_2 conditions (Rubio-Asensio and Bloom 2017). Wang et al. (2013) studied wheat yield and its physiology by increasing atmospheric CO_2 concentration using meta-analysis. The findings indicated that increasing CO_2 considerably raised the grain yield of wheat by 24% with a level of 95% confidence. Recent studies (e.g., Yadav et al. 2019; Hazra et al. 2019) on the East Indian tropical rice system have shown that grain yield increased by 22.6% in the face of high CO_2 (550 ppm), but there is no detrimental impact on reducing grain yield at high temperatures (2 °C more than ambient) in the wet season. Therefore, changes caused by GHG are not only about the negative effects, but may also have some positive effects as well (e.g., maintaining a certain temperature level; blocking the harmful solar radiation). Consecutive and various climatic stresses on crops and the challenge of coping with them cause considerable damage to crop production (Bal and Minhas 2017), requiring considering adequate adaptation approaches. In addition, climate change due to increased GHG emissions is expected to change the quality of grain. Biochemical changes in tissue composition may change interactions of crop-pest in prospective climates. Further, from the phenological aspects, crop performance and product quality are also affected. Because in nature crops are perennial and live under climate change and climate stress, adaptation options needed to be multidimensional.

Climate change also has various effects on livestock and, particularly, on cattle. Increasing humidity and temperatures, for example, lead to heat stress among the animals and consequently to reductions in meat and milk production (Bett et al. 2017). Marine fish are affected by changes in the breeding season, horizontal and vertical expansion of the habitat, and increased breeding cycles and growth rates (Feng et al. 2021). In the future, poultry may be exposed to more heat stress, requiring the development of technologies that help mitigating these effects, such as effective sheds. The overall effects of climate change on livestock health, as well as on the availability of quality feed in sufficient quantities include:

- Increased animal mortality due to heat stress (Feng et al. 2021);
- Reducing access to water, restricting animal access to pastures and disrupting feed production (Bett et al. 2017);
- Contributed to land degradation that lead to less availability of feed (Godde et al. 2021);
- Changes in rainfall patterns, the spread of vector attacks and more outbreaks (e.g., Rift Valley fever virus in East Africa);
- Changes in the pattern of helminth infections due to changes in temperature and humidity (Fox et al. 2015);
- Further spread of vectors in colder regions (malaria) or in warmer regions (bluetongue disease) (Cordeiro et al. 2019);
- Land use changes for crops and fodder and thus reducing the quantity and quality of animal feed and
- Changes in digestibility of feed and plants decomposition with increasing temperature (Oyebola and Olatunde 2019).

Rising sea levels due to climate change have had a significant effect on aquaculture and fisheries. Different environmental conditions are emerging as sea levels rise for aquaculture, coastal fishing, and mangrove ecosystems. Coastal communities are affected by severe weather events, causing damage to infrastructure and floodings of flood-prone rivers. In addition, after harvesting, processing, transportation, and distribution processes are affected, which has considerable effects on livelihoods, food prices, and food security. The effects of climate change on the fisheries sector include:

- Positive impacts
  - In the aquaculture sector, climate change scenarios can positively impact the aquaculture sector due to decreasing the effect of cold weather. Increased growth of aquatic species is expected on warmer nights and winters (Kibuka-Musoke 2007);
  - Reduced costs related to the construction of antifreeze structures and water heating (Oyebola and Olatunde 2019);

  - Unsuitable water for growing crops such as flood water and salt water may be used to produce fish (Lam et al. 2016).

- Negative impacts
  - Changes in fish species in various geographical areas caused by changes in the sea level, as well as increasing floods, temperatures, and droughts (Plagányi 2019);
  - The impacts of global warming on pests, pathogens, and transmission of disease patterns on fish species and aquaculture (Plagányi 2019)

In the twenty-first century, global agriculture has been strongly influenced by global warming. The productivity of global agriculture is predicted to decrease about 3 to 16% by 2080, with an average productivity decline of 10 to 25% in developing countries (Mahato 2014; Malhi et al. 2021). Wealthy countries like Norway and Switzerland will experience a moderately positive impact from an 8% rise in productivity to a 6% decrease (De Pinto et al. 2020). The possible effects of climate change on agriculture vary from region to region. Sub-Saharan Africa (SSA) has been recognized as a highly vulnerable region to climate change. This region hosts the greatest rate of malnourished people at global level, and an important part of the national economies of the region's countries is reliant on agriculture. Additionally, about 85% of the water resources are used for agricultural purposes (Gong et al. 2020) and relatively rudimentary, inefficient farming techniques are very common. Other reasons include droughts (which also affect other parts of the world, such as Asia), and the dominating presence of smallholder production systems that have very limited capacity for climate change adaptation. By 2050, the highest negative effects are expected to appear in areas where the demand for food is high (Fernandes et al. 2012). The deterioration in crop yields in Africa is expected to be around 4–5%, while the increase in demand is estimated to reach 150–228% (Bajželj et al. 2014; Dawit et al. 2020). In North America, food demand is expected to grow by only 38% and crop yields are anticipated to increase by 5% (Iizumi et al. 2017) (Table 4.1).

Importance of CSA

After examining the climate change effect on agriculture, questions arise as to why the CSA is important in regard to mitigation and adaptation to

Table 4.1 Comparison between expected changes in food demand and impacts of climate on food crop yields

Region	*Changes in food demand (%)*	*Impact of climate change on yields*	
		A1 (%)	*B1 (%)*
South Asia	+103	−4	−3
West Asia	+139	−1	−1
East Asia	+47	+2	+1
Western Europe	+10	+3	+4
Eastern Europe	+19	−9	−5
Sub-Saharan Africa	+228	−5	−3
North Africa	+150	−4	−2
Temperate Latin America	+92	+7	+7
Tropical Latin America	+92	−5	−5
Temperate North America	+38	−3	−2
Boreal North America	+38	+5	+6

Source Bajželj et al. (2014)
Note A1[1] and B1[2] are different storylines as described in the IPCC Special Report on Release Scenarios (Nakicenovic and Swart 2000).

climate change. By 2050, the global population is anticipated to grow by 1.3 times, from 7.87 billion in 2021 to 9.7 billion (FAO 2017), and to feed this population, the production of the agriculture sector should be raised by at least 60% (Westermann et al. 2018). Food security is affected by the threats posed by climate change. Therefore, approaches for the adaptation to and mitigation of climate change, i.e., by decreasing GHG emissions are becoming essential. In this regard, the CSA strategies are an effective solution to achieve sustainability, food security, resilience, and efficiency.

[1] The storyline and family of Scenario A1 describes a world of rapid economic growth, a global population that rises and then declines in the middle of the century, and a fast introduction of new and more efficient technologies.

[2] The B1Storyline and Family Scenario describes a convergent globe with the equal population in the world that peaked and then declined in the middle of the century, like the A1 storyline, but with fast shifts in the structure of economic condition toward a service economy and information, by reducing the intensity of materials, and introducing clean technologies with efficient resources.

To understand the CSA approach, it is important to know about its historical development and its dimensions. CSA was developed by the Food and Agriculture Organization of the United Nations (FAO) in 2006 as a unified approach to address the barriers to climate change (FAO 2009, 2017). Then, in 2010, the concept was introduced at the first World Conference on "Food Security, Agriculture and Climate Change" in The Hague (De Pinto et al. 2020). The Second World Conference was held in Hanoi in 2012, and based on the CSA sourcebook (FAO 2013), in developing countries, the issue of supporting smallholder and marginalized farmers and vulnerable people was discussed (Wassmann et al. 2019). The Third World Conference was held in Johannesburg in 2013, marking the beginning of efforts to discuss the CSA Alliance. Finally, in 2014 in New York, the issue of global unity was presented to the CSA Action Plan at the Climate Summit (De Pinto et al. 2020). The summit was aimed at further climate change measures to decrease GHG emissions to decrease mean temperatures at the global level from increasing more than 1.5 °C (2.7 °F) above pre-industrial levels (Summit 2014).

Dimensions of CSA

CSA can be described as an integrated approach to technical development, management and asset to achieve food security and sustainable development in agricultural sector to deal with climate change (FAO 2013; Chandra et al. 2018). The FAO (2015) has also defined the concept of CSA as a way to achieve food security in changing climates. Improving food security is a critical goal of the CSA and helps communities adapt to climate change by adopting proper approaches. This definition indicated that the main goal of CSA is food security and sustainable development, while adaptation, mitigation, and productivity are recognized as three interrelated pillars needed to achieve this purpose (Fig. 4.1) (Mwongera et al. 2017).

Productivity: CSA aims to improve agricultural productivity and increase crop, livestock, and fish yields without adversely affecting the environment, which increases nutrition and food security. The main issue associated with increasing productivity is sustainable development (Mwongera et al. 2017).

Adaptation: CSA aims at reducing farmers' exposure to short-term risks as well as at strengthening their resilience by building capacities to adapt to long-term stresses. Special consideration is paid to the provision

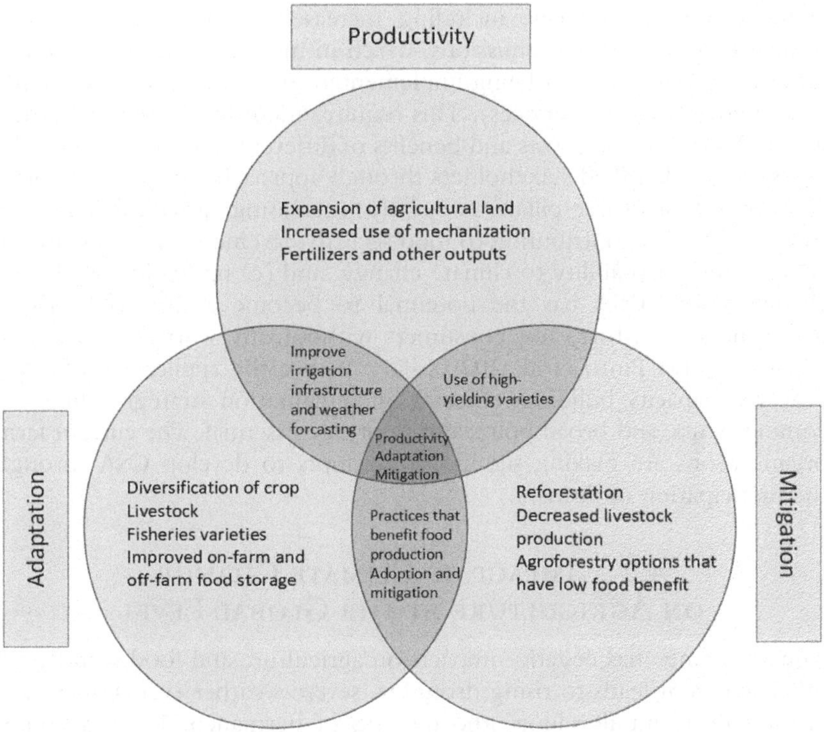

Fig. 4.1 Pillars of CSA with focus on connecting productivity with adaptation and mitigation (*Source* Mwongera et al. [2017])

and conservation of ecosystem services, which are crucial to supporting productivity and the ability to adapt to climate change (Fahad and Wang 2018).

Mitigation: CSA contributes to reducing or eliminating GHG emissions. This also includes the reduction of deforestation resulting from agricultural land expansion, and improved soil management in a way that maximizes the potential for carbon sequestration and CO_2 uptake from the atmosphere (Wassmann et al. 2019).

The CSA approach, contrary to the development of conventional farming methods, systematically integrates the planning and development of sustainable farming systems into climate change. In general, CSAs generate three outcomes, including increased productivity, enhanced resilience, and decreased emissions, which in most cases all three are not achievable. When CSA is being implemented, trade-offs occur frequently (e.g., with ecosystem services). This requires identifying potential synergies and weighing the costs and benefits of different options based on the goals of the identified stakeholders through approaches of participatory.

CSA contains three pillars, namely (a) increasing agricultural productivity and by this contributing to food security, (b) increasing resilience of systems and adaptability to climate change, and (c) mitigation of climate change. Thus, CSA has the potential to become a threefold success for farmers, investors, and consumers without any worries, exchanges, and losers (De Pinto et al. 2020). To enhance the application of CSA, however, capacity building, efficient implementation strategies, financial commitments, and broad political support are essential. The current farm organizations are making significant attempts to develop CSA through the participation of farmers.

4.2 Impact of Climate Change on Agriculture at the Global Level

Climate change has negative impacts on agriculture and food security. In other words, it leads to rising droughts, severe weather events, increased precipitation and floodings, the melting of permanent ice and consequently increasing sea levels, and land degradation processes, among others. Human-induced land degradation occurs mostly in ice-free areas. Coastal areas and arid lands are more exposed to erosion and degradation of lands due to human-induced land degradation. Between 1961 and 2013, the prevalence of drought in arid lands raised by 1% worldwide, affecting approximately 380 to 620 million people in these areas (Hellin and Fisher 2019). Southeast Asia, sub-Saharan Africa, the Arabian Peninsula, and the Middle East were among the most vulnerable to desertification. In particular, the average global temperature has risen by about 1.53 °C, while the global surface average temperature has risen by about 0.87 °C (between the 1980s and 2000s) (Imran et al. 2019). Overall, surface air temperatures (land only) have more than doubled in recent decades compared to pre-industrialization (1750), which in the last century has induced global warming at an alarming pace.

Evidence of Climate Change Across the World

From 1961 to 2003, drought events increased dramatically in the Mediterranean region, Northeast Asia, Africa, and South America (Noll et al. 2020). Observing the global trend in the last five decades, the decrease of polar regions and the expansion of arid regions with increasing global warming is evident. Accordingly, displacement of seasonal activities and changes in the abundance of plants and animals in certain areas were witnessed widely and documented (e.g., Canada and Mexico) (Boone et al. 2018). The incidence of heavy rainfall has increased worldwide. The emergence of vegetation greening in Southeast Australia, North America, Central South America, and Asia was shown by satellite images due to the prolonged growing season, growing nitrogen deposition rate, and fixation and fertilization of carbon dioxide (Allen et al. 2019). In parts of North America, northern Eurasia, and Central Asia, vegetation browning has been detected because of water stress. Global warming is still a dominant trend, but fortunately over the past three decades, remote sensing satellite imagery has shown a relatively large proportion of "Greening of Vegetation" compared to "Browning of Vegetation" worldwide. Coasts are becoming more eroded as sea levels rise, and land use in Africa, Asia, Australia, and the coastal areas of South America is under unprecedented pressure (Nguyen et al. 2021).

Impacts of Climate Change on Agriculture Production

Climate change has adverse effects on the agriculture, forestry, and livestock sector. According to forecasts (e.g., Mall et al. 2017; Mall et al. 2018), food security is undermined due to climate change. It is predicted that by the middle of the twenty-first century and beyond, in tropical and temperate regions for local crops such as wheat, rice, and corn, an increase of about 2 °C will have negative effects on production levels. Rising global temperatures of around 4 °C in most subtropical regions are expected to decrease groundwater and renewable surface water and thus increase food demand, which will pose significant risks to global food security (Araya et al. 2015; Ahmad et al. 2020). It is expected that production of wheat in the world decreases by 6% for each further increase in temperature, and this rate varies in different places and times (Asseng et al. 2015). Extensive studies (e.g., Kongsager 2017; Lobell and Gourdji 2012; Zhao et al. 2017) around the world point to evidence of the effect of climate change on declining yields of crucial cereal crops. In general, the global agro-modeling (e.g., dynamic fuzzy models) literature shows the possible adverse impacts of climate change. Table 4.2 shows some of the reports published to date. Increased variability in rainfall and rising temperatures significantly affect food production. Teixeira et al. (2013) evaluated soybean, rice, wheat, and corn crops affected by climate change. They found that agriculture in subtropical and temperate regions may challenge significant yield reductions due to severe temperature periods. They emphasized the need for agricultural policies, necessary management measures, and the development of adaptation strategies to reduce the effects of heat stress on the global food supply. Ma et al. (2021) predicted climate change scenarios when CO_2 concentrations doubled with the Generation Circulation Model (GCM)[3] and showed that soybean grain yield was reduced in almost all locations. In different scenarios, the average yield reduction varied from 14% in West India to 23% in Central India. In Ethiopia, Kassie et al. (2015) predicted that by 2050, corn yields would decline by 20% due to climate change compared to 1980 and 2009. Similarly, Mulungu and Ng'ombe (2019) describe an adverse impact on the production of maize in sub-Saharan Africa by 2055. According to the findings of He et al. (2018) in China, the effect of climate change on rice yields is very unclear due to the parameters of biophysical processes, severe temperature stress, and uncertainty of climate change scenarios in crop models. They indicate that compared to 1961–1990 levels across the study area, average rice yields may change from 3.0–10.4% until 2020, 2.1–26.7% to until 2050, and 26.4–39.2% by 2080, respectively, in response to water changes, depending on the effects of CO_2 fertilization.

These studies' findings indicated that food systems can be affected by climate change in various ways. These impacts can directly influence crop production and include e.g., changes in rainfall patterns which causes flood or drought, temperature changes (warmer or colder) that lead to shifts during the season of growing, changes in quality and access to groundwater for irrigation, and changes in supply chain infrastructure and consequently food prices. The comparative significance of climate change for food security varies from region to region.

[3] The General Circulation Model (GCM) is a type of climate model that uses the planetary or ocean public circulation for the model (Ma et al. 2021).

Table 4.2 Case studies on the impact of climate change on the production of crop

Crop	*Location*	*Impact on yields*	*Scenario*	*References*
Rice	South Corea	Increase 12.6–22% Decrease 22–35%	CO_2 elevation Temperature	Kim et al. (2013)
	Eastern China	7.5–17.5% 0.0–25% 10.0–25%	2020 2050 2080	He et al. (2018)
	Italy	Increase Constant Decrease Increase	CCSM4 ECHAM6 RCP2.6 RCP4.5	Bocchiola (2015)
	Northeastern China	7.19% 12.39% 14.83%	2010–39 (RCP4.5) 2040–69 (RCP4.5) 2070–99 (RCP4.5)	Zhou and Wang (2015)
Wheat	Northeastern Austria	Decrease 2%, 8%, 7–10%	2020, 2050, 2080	Alexandrov et al. (2002)
	Global South Asia Southeast Asia South America	Decrease (15–45%) Decrease (20–75%) Decrease (10–95%) Decrease (12–27%)	2080	Fischer et al. (2005)
	Europe	Decrease 1.13%, 0.9%, 0.68%	2020, 2050, 2080 (A1F1)	Ewert et al. (2005)
	Europe	Decrease	2050	Olesen et al. (2011), Trnka et al. (2014)
	Australia	Decrease 2–10%	2030, 2060, 2090	Anwar et al. (2015)
Maize	United States	Decrease 0–45%	2050–59	Southworth et al. (2000)
	Sub-Saharan Africa	Decrease 22%	2050	Schlenker and Lobell (2010)
	Europe	Increase	2050	Olesen et al. (2011)
	Central Asia	A1B		Teixeira et al. (2013)

(continued)

Table 4.2 (continued)

Crop	*Location*	*Impact on yields*	*Scenario*	*References*
	Panama	Decrease 0.5% and 0.1%	Near-term A2 and B1	Ruane et al. (2013)

Generally, the rising temperature at the leaf surface can change the efficiency of photosynthesis, decrease yield duration, and increase the rate of respiration for plants (Hatfield et al. 2020). Moreover, evapotranspiration from the canopy of plants, soil, and air increases with rising temperatures and causes mineralization of nutrients in the soil, which may reduce the efficiency of nutrients. Important and indirect consequences of climate change that have an adverse effect on crop productivity include consecutive droughts, soil erosion, low quality of irrigation systems, and more frequent floods. Figure 4.2 shows the potential negative influence of climate change on the crops production.

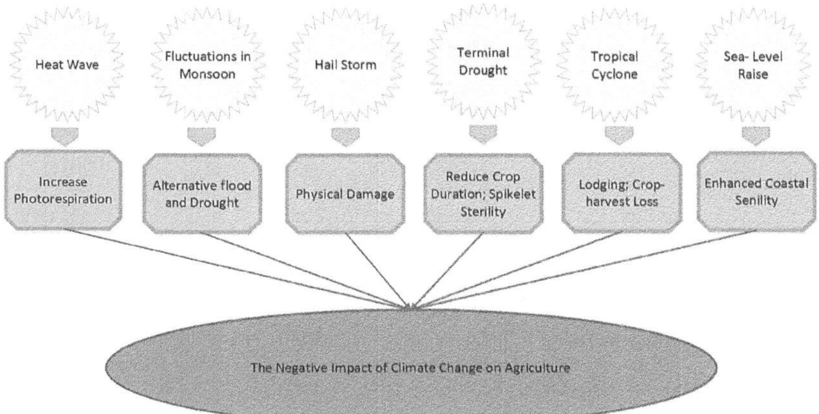

Fig. 4.2 Potential negative effects of climate change on the production of crops (*Source* Hatfield et al. [2020])

Impacts of Climate Change on Ecosystems Services

Climate change jeopardizes many of the advantages of nature or ecosystem services that humans derive from land and water. Climate-induced ecosystem dysfunctions are probable to have outcomes for community dependence on ecosystems for wildlife food, recreation, nutrient cycles, waste processing, natural hazard conservation, and climate regulation among others (Leal Filho et al. 2021). The primary benefits of nature-based services are that they can provide jobs and economic opportunities away from "economic bubbles."[4] In other words, well-managed ecosystems deliver many benefits. These ecosystems provide the basis for sustainable development and a functioning society. Moreover, ecosystem structures and functions offer a variety of services, such as curbing the destructive effects of floods or hurricanes, critical habitats for commercial and recreationally valued species, filtering sediments and pollutants, and carbon storage and separation (Moss et al. 2021). Ecosystem services have many social values that reflect the preservation of human health, livelihoods, and cultural and aesthetic values. Human activities and changing climate affect the provision of these ecosystem services and are of great importance in these changes. Human decisions affect the health of land, coastal and marine systems and their capability to support future generations (Boone et al. 2018). There are various ways to calculate the value of ecosystem services. To determine the effect of changes in an ecosystem function on the production of goods or services, other production functions use statistical analysis to show that a traded resource can be valued utilizing another approach. The main problem with this approach is the accessibility of scientific knowledge or data needed to assess production performance. Information on the demand for ecosystem services and their social value can be combined with biophysical supply estimates to create forecast maps of use and service value. Ecosystem service mapping is crucial to comprehending the ways ecosystems causes human well-being and to supporting policies that affect natural resources. Economic valuation methods consider changes in the supply of ecosystem services as input and turn into changes in human welfare in terms of money. The importance of ecosystem services can be effectively achieved through

[4] The economic bubble represents a situation in which the price of assets is higher than what fundamental underlying factors can reasonably describe.

supporting, provisioning, regulating, and cultural services (Staudinger et al. 2012; Weiskopf et al. 2020).

Difference Between Resilient Agriculture and CSA

The main goal of CSA is to use modern and advances agricultural technologies such as high-yield cultivars, foodstuffs, food supplements, pesticides, high yields, fertilizers, land management and irrigation techniques that lead to resilient systems and high yields (Dong 2021). It is crucial to meet the nutritional requirements of the growing population as well as the economic growth needed to decrease poverty. Thus, inefficient CSA targeting lacks the distinctive livelihood transfer capacities of small-scale farmers, which is related to the facilities and constraints created by different livelihoods. The approaches of CSA also need broader programs, including budget for the building capacity among farming households to make a non-agricultural livelihood (Azadi et al. 2021). The CSA approach integrates conventional and modern practices, technologies and services that are relevant to a special location to adapt to climate change and variability (e.g., extreme events such as tropical storms) (Khatri-Chhetri et al. 2017). This includes the use of Information Communication Technology (ICT) tools, methods of plant and animal breeding, the use of modern and local greenhouses for crop growth, irrigation techniques and innovative production systems for livestock (Kombat et al. 2021). For example, traditional on-farm water harvesting systems, build stacks to store water, fish farming on rice fields, and mixed and cultivation methods. Therefore, new technologies and innovations must achieve all CSA pillars (productivity, resilience, and GHG emission reductions) (Aggarwal et al. 2018).

Climate-resistant agriculture (CRA) is an approach that involves the sustainable use of the existing natural resources through agricultural and livestock production systems to achieve long-term productivity and farm income under climate change scenarios (Anderson et al. 2020). This will reduce hunger and poverty in the face of climate change for future generations (Venkatramanan et al. 2020). CRA measures can change the current situation and maintain agricultural production from the local to the global level, especially in a sustainable way. Improving both the access to and use of technology, transparent trade regimes, increasing the use of resource conservation technologies, increasing the adaptation of agricultural and livestock products to climate stress, are the results of resilient climate approaches (Khatri-Chhetri et al. 2019). Most countries, such as China, Japan, and Russia, are in crisis due to disasters and conflicts, but food security is affected by inadequate food supplies, fluctuations in basic food prices, high demand for agricultural fuels, and sudden climate change (Azadi et al. 2021). In this regard, strategies and technologies for adaptation to climate change are presented, which include: tolerance of crops and livestock breeds to biotic and abiotic stresses, feed management, water management, agro-advisory, soil organic carbon (SOC), and regional, international and national programs for climate change adaptation.

Impacts of Climate Change on Vulnerability

The goal of Vulnerable-Smart Agriculture (VSA) is to understand obstacles in order to improve livelihoods of small-scale farmers (Azadi et al. 2021). VSA seeks to design "participatory" intervention plans that assist farmers overcome obstacles (e.g., technical, economic, political, cultural, and social) to improve their livelihoods. CSA in low-income countries such as Afghanistan, Benin, and Bangladesh, is, however, not able to recognize poverty and reflect the absence of capacities and assets and cannot get out of poverty. Therefore, the primary premise of VSA is that a sustainable livelihood approach is a key prerequisite to raise food production, climate change adaptation, and reduce GHG emissions. Thus, VSA can be viewed as an upgraded tool in the field of climate change (Fahad and Wang 2018). It is necessary for all stakeholders to design appropriate VSA approaches for the region using the existing assets. This involves tangible investments for activities that are productive, such as access to land, other natural sources, financial capital, means and inputs (Schilling et al. 2020). Moreover, it reflects human capacity, social, and political importance (e.g., capability to communicate equally and adequate results in market chains) (Jamshidi et al. 2019).

Moreover, climate change has a considerable effect on livelihoods, especially those that tend to focus mainly on natural resources. Crop and livestock production, as well as fisheries, are widely influenced by changing climates, and thus, climate change can reduce new livelihood opportunities (Ghazali et al. 2021). For instance, the loss of physical capital due to various natural phenomena can restrict the opportunity for agro-tourism, and this can be an opportunity of sustainable livelihood for poor villagers (Rahman and Hickey 2020). Small farmers in the world have a crucial role in the production of agricultural products. Yet, they are among the marginalized and deprived rural societies, and most of them suffer from deprivation and food insecurity. As a result, CSA goals must be aligned with VSA, which mitigates climate change, provides food security, and guides livelihoods of small-scale farmers at the center of any agricultural practices.

4.3 Perspectives of CSA

CSA is defined as an integrated approach that combines scientific, political, and economic measures to achieve adequate production of crops in the face of climate change. This is almost a new strategy to achieve the aims of sustainable development. The CSA consists of three main pillars including (I) a steady agricultural income and productivity increase; (II) resilience and adoption approaches to climate change (III) GHG emissions decrease or elimination. These three pillars are made up by six dimensions as shown in Fig. 4.3 and described below (FAO 2015).

Framework Dimensions of CSA					
Smart-Weather	Smart-Water	Smart-Crop	Smart-Nutrient	Smart-Carbon	Smart-Institution and Knowledge
Rain Gauge	Aquifer Recharge	Stress-Tolerant Varieties	Soil Health Card	Residue Recycling	village-Climate-Risk Management
Automated Weather Station	In Situ Moisture Conservation	Input-Efficient Varieties	Soil Test-Based Nutrient	Conservation Agriculture	Community Nursery
Climate-based Agricultural Consulting	Efficient Application System	Inter-Cropping	Legumes	Tank Silt Application	CHC
Insurance	Drainage	Diversification	Integrated Nutrient Management	Agroforestry	Seed and Fodder Banks
Awareness	IFS	Planting Methods	Coated Fertilizer	Livestock Management	Capacity Building

Fig. 4.3 Framework dimensions of CSA (*Source* Prasad et al. [2015])

Smart-Weather and CSA

Smart-Weather consists of climate awareness in different conditions, insurance of agricultural products based on climate fluctuations, climate-based agricultural consulting services, and permanent reporting of climate parameters (Jaybhaye et al. 2018). For any type of CSA in terms of climate, constant monitoring of agricultural-related parameters such as relative humidity, rainfall, and temperature is essential (Azadi et al. 2021). Therefore, a prerequisite in every village is the creation of a rain gauge. Installing and maintaining an automated meteorological station at the block level can give the system more credibility to provide agricultural consulting services and plan crop insurance plans based on weather conditions that are considered the essential elements of the CSA. Real-time value-added agricultural advice based on climate data to farmers by public or private agencies is crucial. CSA policies should consider crop insurance to compensate for income losses from climate change and weather fluctuation. Marginal and small farmers are among the most vulnerable groups to the outcomes of climate change (Mbuli et al. 2021). Their livestocks are often threatened by heat and cold stress and fragmented farmland that is not efficient enough to produce crops. Hence, weather-based conservation of livestock against severe weather events is a crucial component of the CSA dimension "Smart-Weather" that is often overlooked (Khatri-Chhetri et al. 2017).

Smart-Water and CSA

The main elements of Smart-Water are rainwater harvesting, recharge of aquifers, in situ moisture retention, efficient irrigation systems, management of drainage, and integrated agricultural systems (Imran et al. 2019). Harvesting of rainwater in the watershed through the structures of water harvesting construction is of primary importance. Collected runoff should be used effectively in water harvesting structures in rainfed areas and its use as supplementary irrigation should be extended and promoted by CSA (Paudel et al. 2017). Conservation of in situ moisture is an old notion that is often overlooked in water management in the agriculture sector (Streimikis et al. 2021). Laser leveling of the land, mulching with plant debris, use of hydrogel storage of cover crops in the whole year, use of adequate fertilizer in the soil, and selective soil remediation are efficient technologies that can be followed to maintain moisture in the area

(Morkunas and Balezentis 2021). Sprinkler and drip irrigation systems and planting furrow irrigation bed with proper land leveling is efficient in raising the effectiveness of irrigation water consumption. Drainage networks are valuable for plain ecologies and terrace agriculture in hilly regions (Khatri-Chhetri et al. 2019). In plain ecologies, productivity in agriculture products, efficient use of fertilizers, emission reduction, and weed management are heavily reliant on an effective drainage system. In the future, water will be a scarce resource in climate change scenarios (Gosling and Arnell 2016). In the United States and Brazil, sprinkler irrigation is a very successful maize water management system. In the CSA, sprinkler and drip irrigation systems should be determined for other cereals in areas where there is insufficient rainfall and soils are more penetrable to the delivery system with specific area changes (Khatri-Chhetri et al. 2017).

Smart-Crop and CSA

Food security, agriculture, and livelihood of large numbers of vulnerable populations around the world are threatened seriously by climate change. Severe climate events, increasing levels of sea, global warming (rising temperatures), changing rainfall patterns, frequent droughts, and floods have negative impacts on the production of crop. In addition, the anticipated effects of expected climate change on cereal crops revealed a considerable decline in yield for rice (−35%), wheat (−20%), sorghum (−50%), barley (−13%), and maize (−60%) (Stoerk et al. 2020). Other possible reasons for the decline in crop yields due to climate change include sudden outbreaks of pests, low efficiency of inputs, and reduced biodiversity in crops. Hence, Smart-Crop adaptation strategies are needed to meet these difficulties to ensure food security, sustainable livelihoods, and environmental conservation.

Other suitable options for "smart-crop" include non-biological stress cultivars, selecting varieties with higher input efficiency, intercropping, mixed cropping, variety of cereal-based crops, and changes in planting techniques. Some of them are currently in practice, but will have to be devised again in site-specific scenarios of climate change. Flood-resistant rice, heat-resistant wheat, drought-resistant rice, maize, wheat, etc., frost-resistant maize, lodging resistant rice-paddy (for cyclone hazards), frost-resistant fruits and cultivars of vegetables should be broadly used and adopted in vulnerable areas. Given the nature of climate stresses, numerous stress-resistant cultivars will be smart strategies.

Smart-Nutrient and CSA

The Smart-Nutrient management strategy is addressed by reducing GHGs, increasing system resilience, and ensuring higher production through proper nutrient management. It involves green manure, brown manure, integrated site nutrient management, application of nitrogen based on a leaf color chart, soil test nutrient management, and nutrient management based on a soil health card (Vijayalakshmi and Barbhai 2021). Green manure is an old method in rice in which *Sesbania* species grow in the field for about 40 to 45 days and are incorporated into the soil before the rice is sown, which can provide 25 to 30 kg ha^{-1} of nitrogen for the soil and helps to maintain its physical condition. Co-cultivation of *Crotolaria juncea* or *Sesbania aculeata* with rice as brown manure and the removal of selective herbicides (e.g., ethyl 2,4-D or bispyribac-sodium) at 25 to 30 days after planting decreases weed growing and biomass and fertility are added to the soil (Morkunas and Balezentis 2021). Nutrient management based on a soil health card is an improvement to the management of soil nutrient based on soil testing in agriculture. This is a smart approach to the climate, although it requires strong organizational support for testing and follow-up suggestions.

Smart-Carbon and Energy and CSA

The goal of Smart-Carbon and Energy technologies is to overcome GHG emissions and thus mitigate climate change. They include conservation agriculture (CA), resource conservation technologies, integrated pest management, and agroforestry. These techniques contribute to carbon sequestration and decrease N_2O, CO_2, and CH_4 emissions by 15 to 25% depending on the location, products, or livestock used. CSA in terms of carbon and energy shows zero waste management performance and tillage adoption (Imran et al. 2019). In this regard, the use of second-generation agricultural machinery such as residue composters, electric rice planting, happy seeders, zero-tilled seed drillers, and solar-operated weeders among others, is important and essential for a smart carbon and energy balance of the system (Imran et al. 2018).

Smart-Institution and Knowledge and CSA

To make agriculture smarter from the knowledge perspective, it is necessary to institutionalize maintenance systems and delivery of technology, which is a combination of conventional and novel scientific knowledge. Institutional assistance for innovative technologies for better adaptation is often discussed. Yet, CSA should institutionalize the mechanism for delivering technological innovation. Informal and formal institutions at the village level are generally critical to strengthen existent interventions or initiate new interventions related to agricultural development, including the Village Climate Risk Management Committee (VCRMC). Smart-Knowledge is related to the equality of gender, ICTs, and the increasing capacities of young farmers through on-site education campaigns and awareness. Management of nutrient, pest and disease applications that can be run on mobile devices have become popular today with smart advice in the local language. Smart systems are attractive especially to young people and make the system transparent, offering instant and fast solutions at a minimal cost. CSA plays an important role in overcoming the gender gap in the agriculture sector. A targeted action to fill this gap could be beneficial in promoting climate-responsive women-risk management programs focusing on reducing their labor burden in agriculture, particularly in regions with great climatic risks (Mukherjee and Batabyal 2021). One of the main drivers of CSA are women farmers, who make up 43 to 45%t of the farm labor and are the backbone of agriculture and the economy of rural (Tsige et al. 2020). Hence, CSA must be Smart-Gender as well. Policies related to CSA should involve the extension of women's abilities and skills, equal distribution of assets, credit accessibility, enhanced communication skills, and participation in the processes of decision-making regarding climate change issues, resilience and food security. The three key factors in developing Smart-Knowledge include sufficient training, the development of leadership activities, and the formation of Women's Self-Help Groups[5] (SHG) (Tsige et al. 2020).

[5] There is a self-help group (SHG) called the financial intermediary committee, which consists of 10 to 25 local women in the 18–50 age group.

4.4 Soil Quality, Soil Resilience, and Soil Health in CSA

Understanding the notion of soil quality and evaluation is important for two reasons. First, the misuse and damage to the soil system should be investigated and appropriate management solutions and options should be provided. Second, understanding soil performance capabilities helps detecting further changes in real time. Soil performance capabilities are not recognizable in soil-related tests because these tests are performed at a specific point of time and provide an overview of the soil fertility status. Conventional soil testing is unable to detect the decline of soil properties that cause production limitations (Bhattacharyya et al. 2017).

Concept and Definition of Soil Quality

The quality of soil is essentially the association of physical, chemical, and biological procedures in the soil that facilitate it to perform vital ecological functions (Bhattacharyya et al. 2020a, b, c). These functions essentially include maintaining nutrient dynamics in the soil–plant system, maintaining biodiversity and restoring its functions, regulating the dynamics of solute water flows, detoxification and buffering toxic matters, and maintaining a socio-economic support system (Seybold et al. 2018). Soil quality is a measurement of soil specificity and is a rational assessment of soil performance with consideration to current and future conditions (Salomé et al. 2016).

At first, the soil quality is defined by Pierce and Larson (1993) as "fitness for use" and then Doran and Parkin (1994) as "capacity of soil to function." They provided a broad description of soil quality that includes maintaining the quality of the environment, improving the health condition of plants and animals, and soil capacity for range performance to maintain biological productivity. Based on Thoumazeau et al. (2019), soil quality is "the capacity of a particular type of soil to perform within natural or overseen ecosystem areas, to maintain the productivity of plant and animal, to preserve or improve the quality of water, and to support human health and habitat."

Soil Quality Assessment

The evaluation of soil's ecological performance on a time scale indicates soil quality. Therefore, it requires periodic evaluation. The main aim of soil conservation evaluation is to assess habitat welfare, water improvement, and agricultural efficiency (Arenas-Calle et al. 2021). Current assessment procedures examine soil properties with the performance of integrated management practices. As a result, soil quality assessment is a three-dimensional approach that includes (1) the formulation of appropriate targets for specific soil tasks; (2) the definition of the minimum data set to select indicators; and (3) the definition of soil quality indicators through statistical ranking. According to the management purposes and particular functions of the site, soil quality indicators should be selected. Environmental impacts, social consequences, and on-farm productivity are the main aims of soil management. Moreover, it can address soil erosion, pollution, social and economic factors (Moebius-Clune 2017). Management approaches and purposes, however, vary based on the views of policymakers, land administrators, and other stakeholders. Therefore, soil characteristics should be analyzed to evaluate soil quality indicators that should be based on management objectives. Another crucial task for evaluating soil quality indicators is the selection of indicators (Mukherjee and Batabyal 2021). A minimum set of data is needed to select the indicators, which include physical, chemical, and biological soil methods that are easily measurable and able to detect changes in soil performance, and stakeholder access, and are tailored to farm needs. In the age of modeling and simulation, which is utilized to improve and predict soil quality indicators, minimum data sets must also be sensitive to management practices and climate change (Bhattacharyya et al. 2017). In agricultural studies, mostly principal component analysis (PCA)[6] is used for selecting indicator minimum data sets. Instead of individual preferences, statistical tools for representative observations are used to select a large number of observations (Raiesi 2017). Reducing the number of indicators is one of the main functions of these choices. The selected indicators should represent particular soil performance and may be varied for different yields. After selecting the indicators, the outputs are transferred to the linear or

[6] Principal component analysis (PCA) is a strategy to decrease the dimensionality of such datasets, raising interpretability but at the same time minimizing loss of information (Raiesi 2017).

non-linear scoring procedure. For developing soil quality indices (SQI), indices are first turned to fewer unit numerical scores to determine the limitations for each index. Determining critical constraints for indicators for particular soil type yields is a key factor in SQI (Paz-Ferreiro and Fu 2016).

Soil Resilience and Soil Health

The soil's ability to withstand any return and change to its original state is defined as soil resilience. Mainly, it is associated with the elasticity or extent of recovery, the amplitude or extent of recovery potential, and the hysteresis or pattern of soil recovery (Ludwig et al. 2018). Accordingly, it can be concluded that soil resilience and soil quality are related but differ from each other. Hence, it refers to traction (the amount of recovery), amplitude (the possibility of recovery), and hysteresis (the pattern or path of soil recovering) (Hirsch et al. 2017). In general, soil quality addresses soil performance and ecosystem services, while resilience indicates the soil's ability to recover in the event of stress. Soil resilience can be specified empirically in terms of soil quality (Fig. 4.4).

Various factors affect soil resilience, including biodiversity, climatic conditions, inherent soil properties, water balance, and predominance of materials (Lynch 2015). However, with effective land use management, soil resilience can be significantly increased (Ludwig et al. 2018). Maintaining soil quality is one of the important functions of soil resilience. By maintaining soil quality, soil resilience can be achieved, which creates a win–win relationship for better socio-economic resistance, effective organizational performance, and higher productivity, which can improve soil resilience (Bhattacharyya et al. 2017).

Sustainable Soil and Land Management for CSA

Soil degradation makes the soil vulnerable to the adverse effects of climate change. Soil erosion is accelerated when soil organic matter is degraded from the soil. A fundamental step for CSA is the separation of organic carbon in the soil, since both the potential of sustainable farming products and the resilience of ecosystems increase with the existence of organic carbon (FAO 2015; Mukherjee and Batabyal 2021). With the increase of SOC, a large part of the degraded soil is regenerated and as a result, soil erosion is reduced. Large-scale rehabilitation of degraded soils is

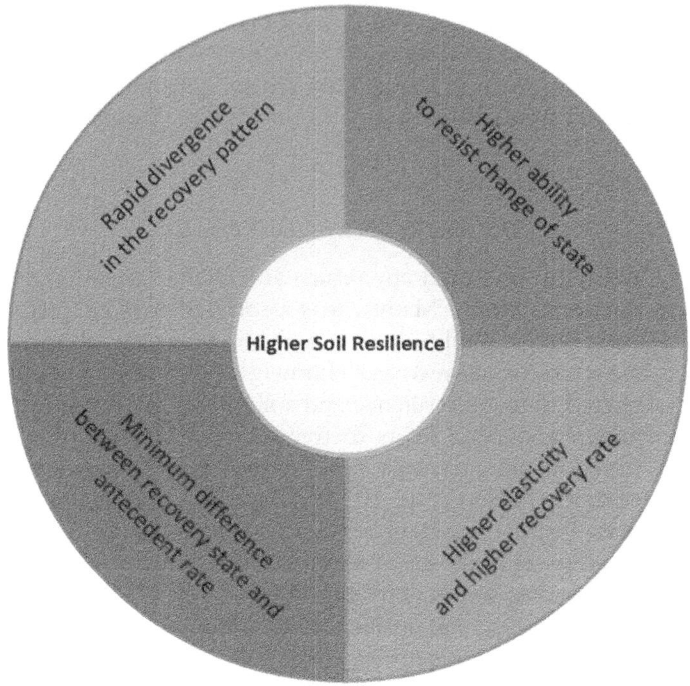

Fig. 4.4 Dimensions of soil resilience (*Source* Hirsch et al. [2017])

essential for soil carbon sequestration and maintenance of soil production potential. The basic criterion for promoting SOC accumulation is erosion reduction (Seybold et al. 2018).

Soil degradation is mostly due to the adverse effects of poor management practices and climate change. With the process of land degradation, soil biodiversity and organic carbon are reduced and as a result, soil erosion occurs more rapidly. Moreover, all these factors increase the vulnerability to climate change. Some of the methods that cause land degradation include intensive cultivation, burning of crop residues, unbalanced and inefficient fertilizer application, and defective irrigation practices. For instance, a study conducted by Zach et al. (2006) in semiarid savanna soils of La Pampa in Argentina showed that due to unsustainable land use change, soil carbon stock fell by about one-third over a five-year period. Cerri et al. (2007) found that establishing pastures in cleared Amazon rainforest can emit about 8 to 12 tons of CO_2 per ha of land. Consequently, unsustainable soil management should be avoided, particularly in areas where SOC reserves are inherently low.

Management of Soil Organic Carbon Stock for CSA

Increasing soil carbon sequestration improves the water holding capacity and increases soil fertility. Therefore, one of the key factors in improving plant productivity is soil carbon sequestration. Numerous factors, such as crop management practices, climate, soil, and cultivation systems, control the rate of SOC sequestration (Jat et al. 2019). With the change of tillage methods, soil carbon sequestration in fine-textured soils is different, while straw incorporation has a higher effect on SOC than tillage in coarse-textured soils. Moreover, if there is not enough organic input in the soil, it may cause losses of SOC. In the United States, for example, the conversion of agricultural land to grassland was the main reason for the average increase in SOC (Arenas-Calle et al. 2021).

Factors such as climatic agronomic zone and the variety and intensity of its use affect soil carbon stocks. SOC enhances the structure of soil by connecting particles of soil to water-resistant aggregates, increasing the capacity of water-holding, infiltration, aeration, and availability of soil nutrients. Thus, in agricultural ecosystems, biological resilience is affected by SOC. In the soil, inorganic and organic carbon pools are the long-lived land stock for carbon. Land carbon sequestration occurs in biomass of plants (e.g., trees) and in soil existence biomass, organic C-resistant soils (e.g., hummus), and subsoil inorganic carbon. No-tillage, diversification of crops, and cover crop use offer nitrogen and carbohydrates and let nutrients to be released slowly from decaying debris, thereby helping the crop grow (Das et al. 2022).

4.5 Water Resource Management and CSA

The global agricultural sector is responsible for roughly 70% of the global water consumption (Berrittella et al. 2007). Therefore, with the prediction of increasing water shortage, one of the main challenges by 2050 is maintaining food security (D'Ambrosio et al. 2018). In addition, over the next five decades, the production in agricultural sector must increase by 60 to 70% to provide adequate food for the growing population

(IPCC 2007, 2014). GHG concentrations may be stabilized by preventive measures, but the rising of the sea level will continue as a result of human activities (Sun et al. 2015; James et al. 2018a, b). Globally, these factors can affect hydrological cycle directly or indirectly.

Impact of Climate Change on the Hydrologic Cycle

Influenced by the interactions between bodies of water, the atmosphere, land systems, and oceans, the climate system is complex. There is a close relationship between the hydrological cycle and climate change, which causes considerable changes in regional water systems. Therefore, there is a necessity for proper measures to adapt and mitigate climate change. The pattern of rainfall, evaporation, demand for crop evapotranspiration, and the occurrence of severe events will change under the changing climate scenarios (Sikka et al. 2018). An accurate and comprehensive estimation of possible future climate scenarios is essential for effective water resources management (Table 4.3).

Climate-Resilient Watershed Management

The place where runoff is discharged through a common point in the drain system is called a watershed (James et al. 2018a, b). The development of a climate-resistant watershed is a necessary adaptation approach to changing climatic conditions. The climate-resistant watershed functions as a reservoir and provides water during periods of no rainfall (James et al. 2018a, b). A weather-resilient watershed also helps to control water-induced soil erosion, decrease loss of carbon resources, and ensure the supply of water for supplemental irrigation. Rehabilitation of natural resources in a sustainable way can be possible with the cooperation and efforts of small and marginal farmers and with integrated watershed management. In watershed management, there are various strategies that help to climate change adaptation and mitigation, namely (FAO 2017):

- Watershed management ensures environmental improvements, livelihood and food security increases, and poverty reduction.
- Compared to individual-centered advantages, this strategy has more social advantages regarding adapting climate change interventions even at the level of household.

Table 4.3 Predicted effects of climate change on various components of the global hydrological cycle

Components	*Predicted effects*
Rainfall	• Increased average atmospheric water vapor since the 1980s • From 1901 to 2005, average rainfall increased in the high northern latitudes, while from the 1970s it dropped by 10 degrees south to 30 degrees north • Around the world, the severity and duration of droughts in tropical and subtropical regions have increased and there is a decreasing trend in soil moisture
Glacier	• The freezing and breaking dates of ice for lakes and rivers have changed • Snow cover and permanent frozen layers have been destroyed • As the Earth's temperature rises, there will be fluctuations in atmospheric vapor pressure
Sea level changes	• Rising global temperatures will cause glaciers and ice sheets to melt, raising sea levels
Changes in the pattern of evapotranspiration	• Changes in potential evapotranspiration due to changes in speed of the wind, moisture, radiation, and temperature • Increasing the concentration of atmospheric carbon dioxide affects the physiological activities of plants • Rising global temperatures will lead to increased potential evaporation
Soil moisture	• Decreased soil moisture in higher latitudes, sub-tropics, and the Mediterranean • Increased soil moisture in Central Asia and East Africa with increasing rainfall
Runoff and river flow	• Changes in precipitation, evaporation, and temperature influence river flow and runoff • Seasonality of the current is influenced by a rise in the current during the peak period or a reduction in the current due to the prolongation of the dry season

(continued)

Table 4.3 (continued)

Components	*Predicted effects*
Impact on groundwater	• About 98% of the world's resources of freshwater are supplied by groundwater and soil moisture, and the status of groundwater is strongly associated with precipitation • Climate change poses a threat to groundwater recharge due to consecutive droughts • With less than threshold rainfall, there will be no net groundwater supply in the future • Aquifer salinity may occur in global warming scenarios due to increased evapotranspiration in arid and semi-arid conditions

Source Lu et al. (2019), Koutroulis et al. (2019)

- In watershed management, groups of stakeholders and institutions operate together to conserve ecosystem services and address issues in a coherent manner.
- This integrated approach contributes to achieving several goals, such as empowering societies to adapt to climate change, reducing GHG emissions, protecting the environment, and securing livelihoods.
- In the context of integrated watershed management, there is a need for a sustainable joint measure with regard to livelihood security, resilience to climate change and mitigation.

Water Management Strategies Under CSA

Climate change is known as a multidimensional approach that makes adaptation strategies a complicated task. For instance, different sectors influenced by climate change are interconnected (water, industries, farming system); there is spatial diversity on a large scale (local, regional, national), and there are different ways of adaptation strategies (physical, policy, technological interventions) also with various climatic zones (arid, mountainous, and polar regions). Water management in stress conditions under CSA can be classified into the allocation of water, water increase, water management based on need, demand and water storage in water

Table 4.4 Climate smart water management practices

Parameter	*Practices*	*Result*
• Drought management	• Wide bed furrow • Raised bed and furrows • Ridge and furrow • Mulching • In situ soil moisture conservation	– Improve water efficiency
	• Farm ponds • Investigate dams and tanks	– Improve water productivity and cultivation intensity
	• Conservation agriculture (CA)	– Protection of resource and sustainability
	• Recharging wells • Percolation tanks	– Improve water
	• Emergency crop planning • Modified planting techniques • Recycling of crop residues	– Raise system efficiency and resilience
• Flood • Storm • Excessive rainfall conditions	• Land formation in vulnerable coastal areas	– Production stability – Raise water consumption efficiency
	• Effective drainage and transmission system	– Increase water efficiency and resilience
	• Introduce flood-resistant crop cultivars	– Increase water efficiency and resilience
	• Integrated agricultural system	– Livelihood security – Increase income

Source Sikka et al. (2018)

drought conditions (Olayide et al. 2016). Management in water-surplus conditions was more concentrated on conservation against river floods and drainage (Table 4.4). There are technological management and policy innovations to enhance the water use efficiency in CSA for sustainable irrigation water management (Lipper et al. 2017).

4.6 Management of Energy and CSA

Energy Shortages and Climate Change

Globally, about 30% of the energy resources are used by the food and agriculture sector, which also produces about 20% of the world's GHG emissions (Lammers et al. 2020). Among the major difficulties the world is facing today achieving sustainability in the energy and food sectors is the most important one. Under the predominant climatic conditions, the production of thermal and hydropower is regulated. This in turn can affect the cost of agricultural products by regulating prices of energy. Therefore, climatic stressors also affect the efficiency of energy production systems. Climate change is affecting different energy sources such as water, wind, solar, and thermal systems. Based on Stuart and Escudero (2017), energy consumption raised from around 11.5 EJ to around 500 EJ from 1860 to 2009, and another 55% increase is projected for 2030 if the current energy consumption rate continues.

Global fossil fuel reserves are declining, and oil is considered a rare commodity since most of its reserves are concentrated in few parts of the world. For this reason, the development of renewable energy sources as a viable alternative to fossil fuels is considered an urgent need (Lesage and Van de Graaf 2016). In addition, one of the key factors causing GHG emissions is the burning of fossil fuels. Therefore, in order to achieve the goals of CSA, it is necessary to manage climate risks along with simultaneously increasing ecosystem productivity and improving energy efficiency to reduce GHG emissions (Radovanović et al. 2017).

Alternative Energy Sources in CSA

To meet the energy needs and control GHG emissions into the atmosphere, there exist various alternative energy management strategies. In this regard, renewable energy has a vital role in mitigating climate change patterns and also offers several benefits (e.g., abundant and always available, cleaner than fossil fuels) (Streimikis et al. 2021). Therefore, renewable energy is a very appropriate option due to providing sustainable energy, reducing environmental risks, causing fewer impacts on human health, and creating social security and a cleaner environment. The potential impacts of climate variables depend on the magnitude of global climate change, and the extent of these effects is unclear. Table 4.5 presents some effective energy management solutions for CSA.

Options for Energy Conservation: Adaptation and Mitigation

Mechanized agriculture is heavily dependent on input energy. Therefore, there is a need to exploit renewable forms of energy while making

Table 4.5 Some effective energy management solutions for CSA

No	*Alternate Sources of Energy and CSA*
1	Replacing specific parts of synthetic fertilizers with organic and bio-fertilizers
2	Encouraging and expanding the use of renewable energy sources such as solar, wind, biofuels, and biomass in agriculture
3	Adopting low fuel consumption engines and efficient maintenance
4	Improving the efficiency of greenhouse heating systems
5	Performing proper insulation for cold storage of perishable agricultural products
6	Introducing and promoting low demand crop species
7	Reviewing and improving food storage and agricultural value chains

Source Streimikis et al. (2021)

optimal use of other non-renewable energy sources. Adaptation strategies contribute to decreasing losses and hazards in the energy system. The energy sector becomes resilient to climate change when strategies and efficient energy management become integrated (Streimikis et al. 2021). In addition, to reduce the carbon footprint, water systems need to be designed in a way that require low energy inputs. Generally, there are various techniques for managing soil and crops, some of which include mulching, crop residue management, conservation tillage, integrated farming practice, and residue management. In addition, integrated power plants and agricultural systems can be good options to achieve energy security resistant to climate change. The production of chemical fertilizers requires a huge amount of energy and as a result, replacing them with organic fertilizers leads to energy savings (Stuart and Escudero 2017). The use of water resources for bioenergy production and the protection of marginal agricultural lands must be considered in the sustainable use of natural resources (Bhattacharyya et al. 2020a, b, c). Sorghum is known in India as a potential bioenergy product. A suitable option is CA, which is done with minimal tillage and saves fuel and energy by reducing the number of operations on the farm. Reduced farm operations and less use of agricultural machinery can reduce GHG emissions. As a result, the use of fossil fuel in energy production to combat climate change must be reduced and energy from renewable sources must be provided (Sarkodie et al. 2020). These measures lead to more resilient energy systems and therefore CSA (Fig. 4.5).

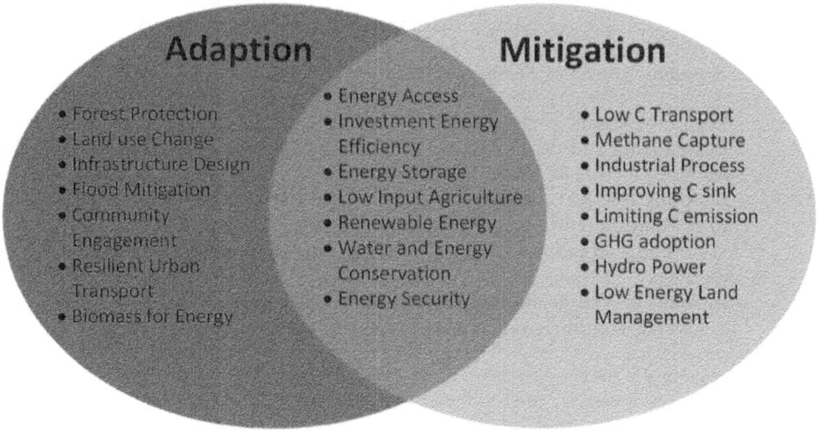

Fig. 4.5 Measures of adaptation and mitigation in energy sector under changing climatic conditions (*Source* Winkelman et al. [2017])

Use of Renewable Energy Sources in CSA

An important factor in CSA is guaranteeing access to environmentally friendly and economic energy sources. Renewable energy is used at various stages of the food system, and to minimize GHG emissions from the use of fossil fuels, the maximum use of renewable energy sources that replace fossil fuels should be promoted (Sarkodie et al. 2020). Significant energy consumption, especially in developing countries, happens along the food value chains, including primary production, storage, and post-harvest processing. Solar and biomass energy among all renewable energy sources have a crucial role in the storage of agricultural products (Martinho and Guiné 2021).

Estimations indicate that with the deployment of solar and wind energy technologies, the replacement of fossil fuels can be achieved with fewer effects on agriculture in about 1.5% of the land currently under agriculture. Currently, renewable energy sources provide 13% of the world's energy needs. According to forecasts by Sarkodie et al. (2020) and Perkins (2012), the share of renewable energy needs to increase to 70% by 2050 to meet the global energy demand. Production costs are expected to decrease in the future with the development of new renewable energy technologies and economies of scale.

4.7 Management of Crop Through CSA

The Importance of Preserving Crop Genetic Diversity in Terms of Climate Change

Conservation of genetic resources is becoming especially important when climate change happens and biological stresses dominate (e.g., pest and diseases) (Altieri et al. 2015). In various climatic conditions, crops with distinct genotypes and different environmental niches show different performances. In a crop species, this diversity causes them to grow under different climatic conditions and in different regions. Therefore, the genetic resources of the crops need to be preserved for the future (Bramel 2021). In agriculture, under different climatic conditions, plant genetic resources have a vital role in creating resilience by providing reserves for future breeding as well as suitable cultivars. Agriculture must adapt to the effects of climate change to feed a growing human population. In this regard, the development of breeds and agricultural species relies heavily on genetic resources resistant to climate stress (Lidwell-Durnin and Lapthorn 2020). To improve product quality to achieve higher performance, it is important to create system resilience and smart use of genetic diversity. In the world, a wide range of genetic diversity, including major crop cultivars, serve as a treasure for plant growers.

Correlation Between Crop Genetic Diversity and Climate Change

Genetic resources for food production and climate change are interrelated. The yield of plant genetic resources and its survival under conditions of climate change are threatened. Therefore, it is vital to use and maintain diverse plant germplasm[7] to meet the challenges of climate change (Kumar et al. 2018a, b). The diversity and yield of crops is heavily influenced by climate change. Climate change affects community structure, distribution, structural diversity of populations, how they respond to biological processes, and functional diversity. Ecosystem dynamics can change under climate change conditions and have implications for the genetic diversity of crops (Ponisio et al. 2015; Rockström et al. 2017).

[7] Germplasm is a living genetic material, such as seed or tissue that is stored for plant breeding, conservation, and other research applications.

Currently, the enormous potential of plant genetic resources can be efficiently utilized for climate change adaptation. For example, by breeding for:

- Fire resistance and tolerance of forest trees
- Tolerance to drought and high temperatures
- Insect tolerance/resistance
- Higher capacity to extract nutrients and water from soil
- Tolerance to flooding and salinity
- Anaerobic seed germination capacity

In the face of climate change, there exists a need for supporting scientific, traditional or local experiences to exploit the maximum potential of plant genetic resources in the agricultural sector (Sofi et al. 2021).

Crop Production Management in CSA

The primary CSA criteria should be considered in smart climate production strategies that include reducing GHG emissions, increasing performance, increasing compatibility, and resulting in system flexibility. These measures include introducing stress-resistant crops, changing the cultivation system in an environmentally and economically sound way, and controlling input sources. The procedures of sustainable crop production previously pursued by farmers with traditional knowledge (e.g., changing farming practices and cultivating adapted crops) are all more important for CSA because they are aware of the balance of the local ecosystem (De Pinto et al. 2020).

It is necessary to understand that CSA (adaptation and mitigation strategies to climate change in agriculture) and "sustainable crops production" are not different and they do not complement each other. Many sustainable crop production strategies, such as integrated farming systems, also have a mitigation component that is fully compliant with the CSA principles. From a broad perspective, both work for the same purpose (Prestele and Verburg 2020). The purpose is to guarantee adequate, safe, and nutritious food for all current and future generations. CSA strategies acknowledge current threats to climate change, crop production, and food security in the future. CSA approaches also investigate the capacity building and resilience of the system for farmers to cope with climate change. Therefore, long-term ecosystem management with cropping patterns is necessary to create system resilience (Jat et al. 2019).

Crop Management Practices Under CSA

Various production methods with the potential for high yield management performance in agriculture contribute to adaptation and mitigation to climate change (Table 4.5). Therefore, the technicality of management practices in CSA is the goal of its introduction. Ecosystem and conservation farming approaches that systematically address resilience are usually appropriate under the CSA.

Conservation Agriculture

Reduction of tillage, preservation of crop residues, and crop diversity are the three key characteristics of CA. CA is CSA and provides sustainable crop performance and facilitates the use of high-yielding species by implementing sufficient nutrients and water. Further, placing the crop residue on the farm constantly enhances the carbon and nutrient status of the soil, which reduces fertilizer use and GHG emissions. CA maintains soil moisture and promotes ecosystem services and resilience (e.g., soil fertility, increased production in the region, and increased sustainable yield) (Ward et al. 2018).

Agro-Ecosystem Approaches

Agro-ecosystems are mainly based on ecological niche, availability of local resources, and vulnerability of farmers. In this approach, the key criteria for selecting crop varieties are low-input use, stress-tolerance, and traditional materials. This pays more attention to ecosystem resilience and farmers' adaptation capacity. Abiotic stress-resistant species of rice, wheat, and maize with modified agricultural practices around the world are promising (Nayak et al. 2018).

Integrated Farming System

An integrated farming system deals with the growth and maintenance of compatible agricultural products (e.g., crops, grasses) and animals (e.g., fish) in the same space (Kumar et al. 2018a, b). An integrated farming system combines crops, livestock, aquaculture, and agriculture and industry as a coexisting system. Therefore, the three CSA criteria, namely increasing productivity, system resilience, and climate change mitigation, are fully in line with the objectives of an integrated farming system. An integrated farming system has advantages that improve the resilience of the system (Babu et al. 2021), namely it:

- Offers a variety of products and decreases the risk of product market fluctuations
- Improves soil chemical, physical, and biological processes
- Promotes less dependency on external inputs
- Ensures labor supply in critical situations
- Creates a buffer against price fluctuations

4.8 Investigating Barriers to the Adoption of CSA

CSA is a suitable strategy to address the current challenges of sustainable agriculture and climate change. In CSA, the interconnections of technologies are as important as any other approach, but their adoption is critical to have a beneficial effect in the long run (Kongsager 2017). CSA adoption depends on the potential of the technology, its efficiency at the level of farm, and farmers' acceptance. Thus, obstacles to CSA adoption can be based on technology or performance of the user (Masud et al. 2017).

Barriers to Agricultural Land Adaptation

Land-based approaches are related to the productivity and resilience/mitigation goals in CSA, which are more focused on mitigating climate change. This approach focuses primarily on afforestation, the use of renewable energy sources, and the growth of crops to produce biofuels (Nguyen et al. 2021). In terms of adaptation, planting cultivars with higher water and nutrient efficiency and at the same time stress-tolerant as well as changing the cropping pattern is recommended (Masud et al. 2017). The land is used to provide ecosystem services, produce products for biofuels, and conserve the biodiversity of resources, and serves as barriers to CSA adaptation. Lack of an obvious policy for water and land rights exacerbates the conflict. Increasing the scale of the mitigation can only be probable by the exclusive use of wastelands or the utilization of residues to produce biofuels. Collaborative approaches to land and water rights for agriculture and energy production can be successful, which can be achieved widely by certifying the use of accepted standards (Nguyen et al. 2021).

In densely populated countries with fewer resources such as China and Ethiopia, land use regulations are more important. In less populous countries with rich resources and less intensive agriculture (e.g., Italy), land-based barriers adaptation of CSA is low. The need to assist and improve field infrastructure, groundwater scarcity, livelihoods and organizational capacity hinder adaptation (Huang et al. 2020). Currently, the preservation of energy, water, biodiversity, and nutrient is low relative to their environmental value. In addition, the low pace at which land use shifts from unproductive food products to fiber, biofuels, and other high-value commercial products are seen as barriers to CSA adaptation. Providing tax breaks and incentives by administration to use almost unproductive land for mitigation targets can decrease barriers to some extent (Cui 2020).

Barriers on the Supply-Side and Demand-Side of Agricultural Supply Chains

Inventors and manufacturers of technologies are on the supply side, while end users of technologies are on the demand side (Luthra et al. 2014; de Janvry and Sadoulet 2020). In developing and developed countries, these barriers are more or less common with regional changes in the components of the supply or demand chain. At the national level, barriers to user supply and demand are controlled by the technology provider for CSA compliance and dissemination through the socio-economic policy program and public vulnerability (Blok et al. 2015). Figure 4.6 shows the barriers to CSA adoption.

Options for Overcoming the Barriers to Mitigation and Adaptation of CSA

For CSA adaptation, options for overcoming economic, social, regulatory, organizational, and behavioral barriers are considered (Table 4.6). Economic barriers can be efficiently reduced by investing properly in commercialization and technology development (Aggarwal et al. 2018). Two effective and beneficial solutions in CSA acceptance are to support

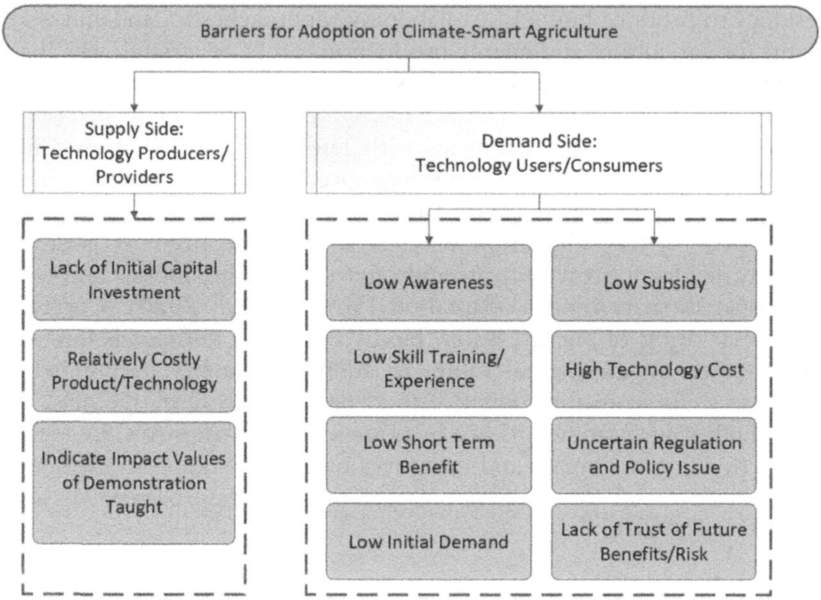

Fig. 4.6 Barriers to CSA adoption (*Source* Blok et al. [2015])

the launch of young entrepreneurs in providing CSA technologies and extending the supply chain of CSA products (Tankha et al. 2020). In the development of products and regulating it, a "user-centric" approach is required to make CSA more efficient and adaptable (Amadu et al. 2020). One effective approach to expanding CSA practices is a bottom-top approach with direct incentives. Local community involvement is also a factor in achieving CSA development plans so that they can choose the goals and path to CSA.. Actual investment in CSA includes the awareness of climate, training to work with CSA equipment, developing skills on a rural level, and persuading rural youth to adopt CSA approaches (Aggarwal et al. 2018).

4.9 Discussion

Adaptation to climate change is considered an essential approach to have a sustainable environment, sustainable development in the agricultural

Table 4.6 Options for overcoming CSA adoption barriers

Barriers	*Strategies*
Economic barriers	Creating a balance between interests (cost ratio of technologies through supply chain)
	Long-term investment through international financial institutions
	Support for startups to innovate and commercialize technology
	Create user-centric/CSA product innovation
	Tax exemptions to research development for production of CSA technologies
Regulatory barriers	User-centric policies and regulations
	Bottom-up approach to technology dissemination
	CSA Business Development
Organizational barriers	Validation of CSA technology on farmers' farms
	Indicate CSA short term profit
	Consider the cost of technology development
Market and consumer-oriented barriers	More access to the consumer
	Upgrade based on CSA specific options consumer section
	Incentives to follow CSA practices
	Systematically priced carbon-saving technologies and ecosystem services
Behavioral and social barriers	Rural youth training and capacity building
	Demonstrate CSA training on the farm in farmers' participation mode
	Direct monetary incentives to follow CSA practices

Source OECD (2014), Wubben et al. (2012)

sector and achieving food security. CSA has an essential role in adapting to climate change. Generally, for the wider implementation of any climate policy or CSA, there is a need for sustainable water and soil management, proper integration of stress-resistant cultivars, improved skills, general dissemination of climate knowledge, and establishment of transparent organizational policies and structures (Alexandrov et al. 2002). There are a number of factors that are considered to be the backbone of CSA adaptation, including technology innovations, weather-related institutions and policies, climate insurance, crop insurance, incentives for ecosystem services, and community participatory approaches to deal with sudden climate risks (Totin et al. 2018). National policies vary from country to country to address climate change issues. Yet, there is a requirement for higher coherence, consistency, and coordination between different levels of organizations to implement CSA in the world (Azadi et al. 2021; Bhattacharyya et al. 2020a, b, c).

Reliance on this system is essential in agriculture by making proper link between climate change and global food security challenges. In this regard, the whole system of conversion from "provider-centric" to "user-centric" is required. The key to CSA adaptation is the practical participation of farmers in CSA technologies in compliance with the "Government Climate Policy" (Feng et al. 2021). In summary, CSA compliance must be examined at the level of the conversion system to provide justice for complicated issues such as hunger, livelihood, poverty, malnutrition, economy, sustainability, and the environment in the status of climate change (Hellin and Fisher 2019). It is the public commitment of society to reduce climate change because we in society are "donors" and "acceptors" of the risks associated with climate change. Vulnerability varies in the current capacity of society to cope with it, but "capacity to cope" is a relative term that is very fragile in the face of climate change. Thus, there is a need for a comprehensive policy that addresses the interests of individuals in vulnerable areas by providing equal opportunities for children, women, and poor communities around the world (Kogo et al. 2021).

The VSA, as a smart system, has the possibility to anticipate crucial events in agriculture, estimate the outcomes of these events, evaluate farmers' livelihoods, and deal with such events. The final objective of the VSA is for marginal and small-scale farmers to be able to actively mitigate climate change and other significant agricultural events that may result in considerable crop losses in agricultural and food production systems (Azadi et al. 2021). CSA activities at the national level are related to a number of subjects that, if not solved appropriately, can undermine the quality of decisions made (Brandt et al. 2017). First, relevant stakeholders should engage with expertise and decision-making. Second, considering an enormous number of criteria when prioritizing and choosing CSA approaches can cause high complexity and uncertainty. Third, valid quantitative and precise spatial data are needed to recognize proper areas to target special CSA practices (Totin et al. 2018).

In this regard, the VSA is recommended as an efficient CSA development that examines adaptation and mitigation measures at the farmer level and evaluates approaches to tackling climate change and food security challenges. It aims to overcome the vulnerability of marginal and small farmers to climate change by increasing the adaptive capacities of agricultural systems to climate stress and thus ensuring food security while reducing GHG emissions from land use change and practices of agriculture. Consequently, as a supplement to CSA, the notion of VSA contains short-term (adaptation) and long-term (mitigation) insights that could be considered in appropriate processes of planning for marginal and small farmers. The demand-based approach, as proposed by the VSA, should be adopted by incorporating the concept of vulnerability into the CSA, meaning that climate change in more vulnerable areas requires more immediate intervention to increase their adaptation capacity. Consequently, information on social, economic, and biophysical dimensions must be considered when planning where VSA practices are suitable.

Although the basic tenets of "sustainable agricultural development" and "smart agriculture with climate" are the same, the CSA needs slightly more policies on reduction, flexibility, and adaptation. Strategies of CSA should be included in the main national agricultural policy plans and the potential of natural resources and the current financial status of the nations concerned should be taken into account. The mainstream CSA policy should be based on a valid national database, people's vulnerabilities, forecasts of climate change, the country's current socio-political situation, obstacles to adaptation, and the country's potential to deal with the future environmental and economic barriers. Therefore, policies related to CSA should be multi-sectoral and integrated, including food security, poverty reduction, growth in economic, GHGs emission mitigation, and system resilience.

CSA Effective and Acceptable Policies

Globally, regardless of resource-rich or resource-poor nations, there are three characteristics that can make CSA more sufficient and acceptable. These features include:

i. Through incentives, productivity-adaptation-reduction is linked to climate change
ii. Priced ecosystem services resulting from CSA practices; and

iii. Regulations for CSA-adoption (Fig. 4.7)

CSA-related policies that connect productivity with adaptation and mitigation of climate change and provide motivation and incentives for holistic strategies have been successful. CSA implementation policies aimed at the pricing of ecosystem services are an important factor in CSA policies (Chandra et al. 2018). Quantification, valuation, and pricing of profits should be done in the short, medium, and long term. Rewards and incentives should be provided through transparent, trusted systems or in cash, encouraging farmers or stakeholders to follow CSA practices while compensating for apparent losses that may result from the loss of subsidies (Lipper and Zilberman 2018). For those using CSA practices, financing should be encouraged instead of general subsidies for the use of inputs in agriculture. Since most CSA strategies are long-term in nature, governments, NGOs, local agencies, and farmers need to cooperate. CSA adoption regulations are one of the most important and fundamental strategies. While CSA practices are extensively adopted, national regulations are required to maintain food security and public interest at the local level.

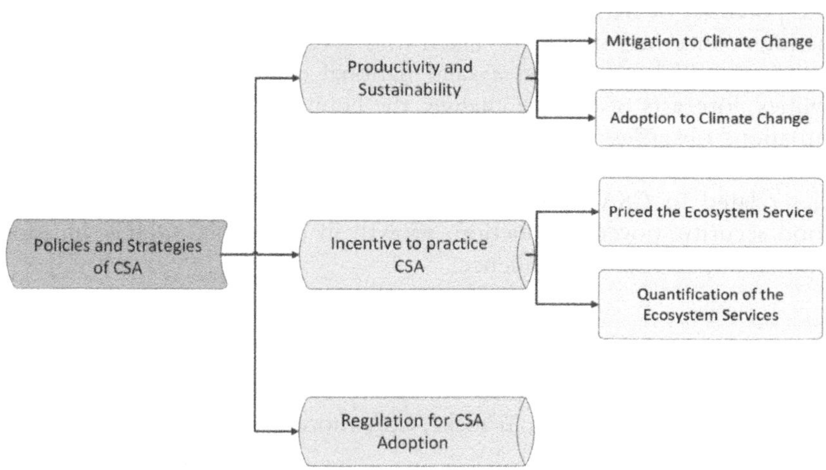

Fig. 4.7 Policies of the CSA Strategy (*Source* Faling et al. [2018])

CSA Monitoring and Assessment

In general, it is not easy to assess and monitor CSA procedures or CSA policies. The effects of CSA are mainly long term and related to environmental issues. In addition, CSA has long-term local and national beneficial effects that are global in nature in terms of climate/environment. Some aspects of CSA have beneficial effects, including increased resilience, increased system efficiency, and reduced GHG emissions (Lipper and Zilberman 2018). Therefore, the criteria for assessing, evaluating, and monitoring CSA and CSA policies over time should be multidimensional to cover multiple sections and locations. CSA assessment procedures should be performed in a short, medium, and long term. Moreover, monitoring of CSA should be associated with current evaluation systems for the development of climate change mitigation and adaptation in agriculture. Multi-criteria assessment should be based on four main aspects, which are sustainable productivity, rising resilience, adaptability, and reducing vulnerability and GHG emissions or climate change (Wassmann et al. 2019). Productivity may be evaluated based on the short and medium term (Taneja et al. 2019). Productivity evaluation should not be an individual or single crop approach but should follow a systemic approach. To evaluate some indicators, a partial yield index and sustainable productivity index can be used instead of evaluating simple crop yields (Olhoff and Christensen 2017).

Resilience is the second most widely used CSA assessment criterion that can be examined from a physical, social, and economic perspective (Lipper et al. 2017). In the mid to long term, system resilience is measured. In particular, the resilience of a system refers to the rapid comeback of the system in its initial condition after it was prone to stress. Assessing the economic resilience of systems can be characterized by criteria such as improving public health, training, livelihoods, level of income, and employment opportunities. Increased income diversity, gender equality, health marketing information among others, are also considered in the social assessment (Venkatramanan et al. 2020). Increasing the social resilience of the system is illustrated by increasing knowledge, technical abilities, social networks, and the way in which the public and farmers administer information, particularly on climate and markets. A significant indicator for assessing CSA is the decrease of vulnerability due to CSA practices adaptation. Increasing adaptation or decreasing vulnerability can be used intermittently to judge CSA efficiency. The CSA approach becomes a new and unique approach by combining mitigation strategies with adaptability and resiliency. Therefore, for CSA assessment, mitigation measures must be identified (Taylor 2018). Other key criteria for assessment are reduced GHG emissions or the potential to mitigate global warming. Production in the agriculture system and economy are also crucial elements of CSA in terms of sustainable development; therefore, the mitigation can also be assessed by the intensity of greenhouse gas emissions (Fig. 4.8) (Venkatramanan et al. 2020).

4.10 Conclusion

The concept of CSA was used in 2009 and aims to improve adaptation and mitigation measures in agriculture to increase their integration and create favorable conditions for improving food security and supporting sustainable agricultural development. The immediate adoption of the CSA after its introduction and launch reflects the need for a framework to guide technical interventions and agricultural policies that demonstrate the importance of the agricultural sector in achieving food security. However, the widespread acceptance of the term CSA before the development of the formal conceptual and methodological framework has led to considerable variation in the meanings used in the term, which has also been debated.

Sustainable agricultural development and CSA have the same principles. However, CSA needs more measures on adaptation, mitigation, and resilience. In addition, CSA processes should be part of the main national policies in agriculture, which should take into account the potential of natural resources and the current financial situation of the nations concerned. CSA's core orientation policies should be according to a valid national database of vulnerabilities, signs and forecasts of climate change, the existing political and social state of countries, challenges to adaptation, and the capacity of countries to meet the environmental and future economic challenges. CSA-related policies should be multisectoral as well as integrated, with approaches such as economic growth, poverty reduction, food security, GHG emissions mitigation, and system resilience. The policy framework may be developed centrally, but implemented locally and in a decentralized manner, maintaining all public and private organizations. These policies should also have milestones and goals and milestones at different time intervals.

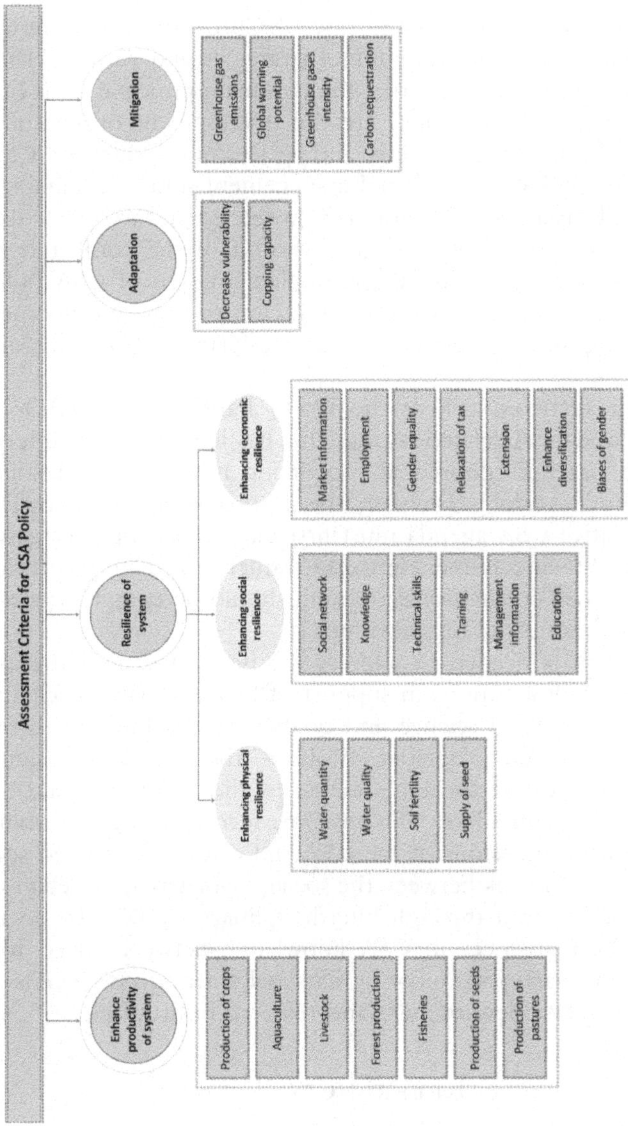

Fig. 4.8 Criteria for multi-sectoral evaluation and monitoring of CSA policies (*Source* Wassmann et al. [2019])

CSA-related approaches have been altered through the input and interconnection of several stakeholders involved in the development and performance of this concept. In the case of CSA, however, differences remain regarding sustainable agricultural strategies and climate change. In particular, in developing countries, the two main principal areas of the ongoing conflict in relevant policy are the development of agricultural development technologies, financing, and agricultural reduction. CSA is a tool for identifying local agricultural management solutions suitable for food security and sustainable development in the agriculture sector under climate change and does not provide a version of the conflict resolution approach to any user. Finally, the implementation of CSA policies based on their significance in incorporating climate change outcomes in sustainable development in agriculture sector efforts in the region will be considered.

Development agencies such as the World Bank and the FAO have strongly influenced CSA-related issues. This has led to various interpretations of CSA practices desired at mobilizing new financial resources for the agricultural sector. However, the co-production of knowledge and a transformative CSA agenda must first target the empowerment of the most vulnerable and farmer networks, rather than elite institutional programs. Top-down conventional research should be complemented by community-based nonprofit organizations.

Further research is needed to address the issue of scale and explain differences in CSA descriptions in support of broad social participation. The obvious gap between science and politics can be bridged through interdisciplinary research programs. Globally, the agenda of scientific research needs to redirect the investments to the "on-farm" and "off-farm" realities of smallholders. This involves reconsidering the political and organizational dimensions of the CSA and can be performed somewhat by reinforcing the link between the social, managerial, and economic measurements of research through interdisciplinary studies. To do this, current production practices in CSA knowledge networks need to be modified with the participation of agricultural institutions, NGOs and executives beyond elite development and research institutions.

References

Aggarwal, P.K.; A. Jarvis; B.M. Campbell; R.B. Zougmoré; A. Khatri-Chhetri; S.J. Vermeulen; A.M. Loboguerrero; L.S. Sebastian; J. Kinyangi; and O.

Bonilla-Findji. 2018. The climate-smart village approach: framework of an integrative strategy for scaling up adaptation options in agriculture.

Ahmad, I.; B. Ahmad; K. Boote; and G. Hoogenboom. 2020. Adaptation strategies for maize production under climate change for semi-arid environments. *European Journal of Agronomy* **115:126040**.

Alexandrov, V.; J. Eitzinger; V. Cajic; and M. Oberforster. 2002. Potential impact of climate change on selected agricultural crops in north-eastern Austria. *Global Change Biology* **8:372–389**.

Allen, M.; P. Antwi-Agyei; F. Aragon-Durand; M. Babiker; P. Bertoldi; M. Bind; S. Brown; M. Buckeridge; I. Camilloni; and A. Cartwright. 2019. Technical Summary: Global warming of 1.5° C. An IPCC Special Report on the impacts of global warming of 1.5° C above pre-industrial levels and related global greenhouse gas emission pathways, in the context of strengthening the global response to the threat of climate change, sustainable development, and efforts to eradicate poverty.

Altieri, M.A.; C.I. Nicholls; A. Henao; and M.A. Lana. 2015. Agroecology and the design of climate change-resilient farming systems. *Agronomy for Sustainable Development* **35:869–890**.

Amadu, F.O.; P.E. McNamara; and D.C. Miller. 2020. Understanding the adoption of climate-smart agriculture: A farm-level typology with empirical evidence from southern Malawi. *World Development* **126:104692**.

Anderson, R.; P.E. Bayer; and D. Edwards. 2020. Climate change and the need for agricultural adaptation. *Current Opinion in Plant Biology* **56:197–202**.

Anwar, M.R.; D. Li Liu; R. Farquharson; I. Macadam; A. Abadi; J. Finlayson; B. Wang; and T. Ramilan. 2015. Climate change impacts on phenology and yields of five broadacre crops at four climatologically distinct locations in Australia. *Agricultural Systems* **132:133–144**.

Araya, A.; G. Hoogenboom; E. Luedeling; K.M. Hadgu; I. Kisekka; and L.G. Martorano. 2015. Assessment of maize growth and yield using crop models under present and future climate in southwestern Ethiopia. *Agricultural and Forest Meteorology* **214:252–265**.

Arenas-Calle, L.N.; J. Ramirez-Villegas; S. Whitfield; and A.J. Challinor. 2021. Design of a Soil-based Climate-Smartness Index (SCSI) using the trend and variability of yields and soil organic carbon. *Agricultural Systems* **190:103086**.

Asseng, S.; F. Ewert; P. Martre; R.P. Rötter; D.B. Lobell; D. Cammarano; B.A. Kimball; M.J. Ottman; G. Wall; and J.W. White. 2015. Rising temperatures reduce global wheat production. *Nature Climate Change* **5:143–147**.

Azadi, H.; S.M. Moghaddam; S. Burkart; H. Mahmoudi; S. Van Passel; A. Kurban; and D. Lopez-Carr. 2021. Rethinking resilient agriculture: From climate-smart agriculture to vulnerable-smart agriculture. *Journal of Cleaner Production*:**128602**.

Babu, S.; K. Mohapatra; A. Das; G. Yadav; R. Singh; P. Chandra; R. Avasthe; A. Kumar; M.T. Devi; and V.K. Singh. 2021. Integrated farming systems: Climate-resilient sustainable food production system in the indian himalayan region. In *Exploring synergies and trade-offs between climate change and the sustainable development goals*, 119–143: Springer.

Bajželj, B.; K.S. Richards; J.M. Allwood; P. Smith; J.S. Dennis; E. Curmi; and C.A. Gilligan. 2014. Importance of food-demand management for climate mitigation. *Nature Climate Change* **4:924–929**.

Bal, S.K. and P.S. Minhas. 2017. Atmospheric stressors: Challenges and coping strategies. In *Abiotic stress management for resilient agriculture*, 9–50: Springer.

Berrittella, M.; A.Y. Hoekstra; K. Rehdanz; R. Roson; and R.S. Tol. 2007. The economic impact of restricted water supply: A computable general equilibrium analysis. *Water Research* **41:1799–1813**.

Bett, B.; P. Kiunga; J. Gachohi; C. Sindato; D. Mbotha; T. Robinson; J. Lindahl; and D. Grace. 2017. Effects of climate change on the occurrence and distribution of livestock diseases. *Preventive Veterinary Medicine* **137:119–129**.

Bhattacharyya, P.; S. Padhy; M. Shahid; P. Dash; A. Nayak; and B. Gangaiah. 2017. Soil quality index under organic farming: Not Available.

Bhattacharyya, P.; H. Pathak; and S. Pal. 2020a. Dimensions of climate-smart agriculture. In *Climate smart agriculture*, 33–39: Springer.

Bhattacharyya, P.; H. Pathak; and S. Pal. 2020b. Energy management for climate-smart agriculture. In *Climate smart agriculture*, 73–84: Springer.

Bhattacharyya, P.; H. Pathak; and S. Pal. 2020c. Soil management for climate-smart agriculture. In *Climate smart agriculture*, 41–56: Springer.

Blok, V.; T.B. Long; A.I. Gaziulusoy; N. Ciliz; R. Lozano; D. Huisingh; M. Csutora; and C. Boks. 2015. From best practices to bridges for a more sustainable future: Advances and challenges in the transition to global sustainable production and consumption: Introduction to the ERSCP stream of the Special volume. *Journal of Cleaner Production* **108:19–30**.

Bocchiola, D. 2015. Impact of potential climate change on crop yield and water footprint of rice in the Po valley of Italy. *Agricultural Systems* **139:223–237**.

Boone, R.B.; R.T. Conant; J. Sircely; P.K. Thornton; and M. Herrero. 2018. Climate change impacts on selected global rangeland ecosystem services. *Global Change Biology* **24:1382–1393**.

Bramel, P. 2021. Key issues facing genebanks in preserving crop genetic diversity ex situ: overview of the range of challenges. *Plant Genetic Resources*:**139–153**.

Brandt, P.; M. Kvakić; K. Butterbach-Bahl; and M.C. Rufino. 2017. How to target climate-smart agriculture? Concept and application of the consensus-driven decision support framework "targetCSA". *Agricultural Systems* **151:234–245**.

Cerri, C.; M. Easter; K. Paustian; K. Killian; K. Coleman; M. Bernoux; P. Falloon; D. Powlson; N. Batjes; and E. Milne. 2007. Predicted soil organic carbon stocks and changes in the Brazilian Amazon between 2000 and 2030. *Agriculture, Ecosystems & Environment* **122:58–72**.

Chandra, A.; K.E. McNamara; and P. Dargusch. 2018. Climate-smart agriculture: Perspectives and framings. *Climate Policy* **18:526–541**.

Cordeiro, M.R.; A. Rotz; R. Kroebel; K.A. Beauchemin; D. Hunt; S. Bittman; K.M. Koenig; and D.B. McKenzie. 2019. Prospects of forage production in northern regions under climate and land-use changes: A case-study of a dairy farm in Newfoundland, Canada. *Agronomy* **9:31**.

Cui, X. 2020. Climate change and adaptation in agriculture: Evidence from US cropping patterns. *Journal of Environmental Economics and Management* **101:102306**.

D'Ambrosio, E.; A.M. De Girolamo; and M.C. Rulli. 2018. Assessing sustainability of agriculture through water footprint analysis and in-stream monitoring activities. *Journal of Cleaner Production* **200:454–470**.

Das, S.; S. Chatterjee; and J. Rajbanshi. 2022. Responses of soil organic carbon to conservation practices including climate-smart agriculture in tropical and subtropical regions: A meta-analysis. *Science of The Total Environment* **805:150428**.

Dawit, M.; M.O. Dinka; and O.T. Leta. 2020. Implications of adopting drip irrigation system on crop yield and gender-sensitive issues: The case of Haramaya District, Ethiopia. *Journal of Open Innovation: Technology, Market, and Complexity* **6:96**.

de Janvry, A. and E. Sadoulet. 2020. Using agriculture for development: Supply- and demand-side approaches. *World Development* **133:105003**.

De Pinto, A.; N. Cenacchi; H.-Y. Kwon; J. Koo; and S. Dunston. 2020. Climate smart agriculture and global food-crop production. *PLoS One* **15:e0231764**.

Dong, L. 2021. Toward resilient agriculture value chains: Challenges and opportunities. *Production and Operations Management* **30:666–675**.

Doran, J.W. and T.B. Parkin. 1994. Defining and assessing soil quality. *Defining Soil Quality for a Sustainable Environment* **35:1–21**.

Ewert, F.; M. Rounsevell; I. Reginster; M. Metzger; and R. Leemans. 2005. Future scenarios of European agricultural land use: I. Estimating changes in crop productivity. *Agriculture, Ecosystems & Environment* **107:101–116**.

Fahad, S. and J. Wang. 2018. Farmers' risk perception, vulnerability, and adaptation to climate change in rural Pakistan. *Land Use Policy* **79:301–309**.

Faling, M.; R. Biesbroek; and S. Karlsson-Vinkhuyzen. 2018. The strategizing of policy entrepreneurs towards the Global Alliance for Climate-Smart Agriculture. *Global Policy* **9:408–419**.

FAO. 2009. Food security and agricultural mitigation in developing countries: Options for capturing synergies FAO Rome http://www.fao.org/docrep/012/i1318e/i1318e00.pdf.

FAO. 2013. Climate-smart agriculture-sourcebook. E-ISBN978-92-5-107721-4.

FAO. 2015. The United Nations (2015) AQUASTATDFO. AQUASTAT, (Database). https://data.fao.org/ref/75f7d9c5-57ab-4a62-88d3-1e47fb50c45.

FAO. 2017. Integrating climate change adaptation and mitigation into the watershed management approach in Eastern Africa: Discussion paper and good practices booklet. **66**.

Feng, X.; H. Qiu; J. Pan; and J. Tang. 2021. The impact of climate change on livestock production in pastoral areas of China. *Science of The Total Environment* **770:144838**.

Fernandes, E.; A. Soliman; R. Confalonieri; M. Donatelli; and F. Tubiello. 2012. Climate change and agriculture in Latin America, 2020–2050: Projected impacts and response to adaptation strategies.

Fischer, G.; M. Shah; F. N. Tubiello; and H. Van Velhuizen. 2005. Socio-economic and climate change impacts on agriculture: An integrated assessment, 1990–2080. *Philosophical Transactions of the Royal Society B: Biological Sciences* **360:2067–2083**.

Fox, N.J.; G. Marion; R.S. Davidson; P.C. White; and M.R. Hutchings. 2015. Climate-driven tipping-points could lead to sudden, high-intensity parasite outbreaks. *Royal Society Open Science* **2:140296**.

Ghazali, S.; H. Azadi; K. Janečková; P. Sklenička; A. Kurban; and S. Cakir. 2021. Indigenous knowledge about climate change and sustainability of nomadic livelihoods: Understanding adaptability coping strategies. *Environment, Development and Sustainability*:**1–25**.

Godde, C.; D. Mason-D'Croz; D. Mayberry; P.K. Thornton; and M. Herrero. 2021. Impacts of climate change on the livestock food supply chain; A review of the evidence. *Global Food Security* **28:100488**.

Gong, X.; H. Zhang; C. Ren; D. Sun; and J. Yang. 2020. Optimization allocation of irrigation water resources based on crop water requirement under considering effective precipitation and uncertainty. *Agricultural Water Management* **239:106264**.

Gosling, S.N. and N.W. Arnell. 2016. A global assessment of the impact of climate change on water scarcity. *Climatic Change* **134:371–385**.

Hatfield, J.L.; J. Antle; K.A. Garrett; R.C. Izaurralde; T. Mader; E. Marshall; M. Nearing; G. Philip Robertson; and L. Ziska. 2020. Indicators of climate change in agricultural systems. *Climatic Change* **163:1719–1732**.

Hazra, S.; D.K. Swain; and P.B.S. Bhadoria. 2019. Wheat grown under elevated CO2 was more responsive to nitrogen fertilizer in Eastern India. *European Journal of Agronomy* **105:1–12**.

He, L.; J. Cleverly; B. Wang; N. Jin; C. Mi; D. Li Liu; and Q. Yu. 2018. Multi-model ensemble projections of future extreme heat stress on rice across southern China. *Theoretical and Applied Climatology* **133:1107–1118**.

Hellin, J. and E. Fisher. 2019. Climate-smart agriculture and non-agricultural livelihood transformation. *Climate* **7:48**.

Hirsch, P.R.; D. Jhurreea; J.K. Williams; P.J. Murray; T. Scott; T.H. Misselbrook; K.W. Goulding; and I..M. Clark. 2017. Soil resilience and recovery: Rapid community responses to management changes. *Plant and Soil* **412:283–297**.

Huang, K.-C.; C.-J. Lee; S.-L. Chan; and C.-H. Tai. 2020. Vulnerability assessment and adaptation strategies for the impact of climate change on agricultural land in Southern Taiwan. *Sustainability* **12:4637**.

Iizumi, T.; J. Furuya; Z. Shen; W. Kim; M. Okada; S. Fujimori; T. Hasegawa; and M. Nishimori. 2017. Responses of crop yield growth to global temperature and socioeconomic changes. *Scientific Reports* **7:1–10**.

Imran, M.A.; A. Ali; M. Ashfaq; S. Hassan; R. Culas; and C. Ma. 2018. Impact of Climate Smart Agriculture (CSA) practices on cotton production and livelihood of farmers in Punjab, Pakistan. *Sustainability* **10:2101**.

Imran, M. A.; A. Ali; M. Ashfaq; S. Hassan; R. Culas; and C. Ma. 2019. Impact of climate smart agriculture (CSA) through sustainable irrigation management on Resource use efficiency: A sustainable production alternative for cotton. *Land Use Policy* **88:104113**.

IPCC. 2007. Summary for policymakers. In: Solomon S, Qin D, Manning M, Chen Z, Marquis M, Averyt KB, Tignor M, Miller HL (eds) Climate change 2007: The physical science basis. Contribution of working group I to the fourth assessment report of the intergovernmental panel on climate change. Cambridge University Press, Cambridge, UK and New York, USA.

IPCC. 2014. Synthesis report. In: Pachauri RK, Allen MR, Barros VR, Broome J, Cramer W, Christ R et al (eds) Climate change 2014: Synthesis report. Contribution of working groups I, II and III to the fifth assessment report of the intergovernmental panel on climate change, p 151.

James, A.; A. Bahadur; S. Verma; P. Reid; and S. Biswas. 2018a. Climate-resilient water management: An operational framework from South Asia. *Learning paper*. IWMI.

James, A.; A.V. Bahadur; S. Verma; P. Reid; and S. Biswas. 2018b. Climate-resilient water management: an operational framework from south asia. *ACT learning paper*.

Jamshidi, O.; A. Asadi; K. Kalantari; H. Azadi; and J. Scheffran. 2019. Vulnerability to climate change of smallholder farmers in the Hamadan province, Iran. *Climate Risk Management* **23:146–159**.

Jat, H.; A. Datta; M. Choudhary; P.C. Sharma; A. Yadav; V. Choudhary; M. Gathala; M.L. Jat; and A. McDonald. 2019. Climate smart agriculture practices improve soil organic carbon pools, biological properties and crop productivity in cereal-based systems of North-West India. *Catena* **181:104059**.

Jaybhaye, P.; N. Deore; and P. Shinde. 2018. Agromet advisory bulletin—A weather smart agriculture technology option for adaptation and mitigation of changing climate. *International Journal of Current Microbiology and Applied Sciences* **7:2644–2653**.

Kassie, B.T.; S. Asseng; R.P. Rotter; H. Hengsdijk; A.C. Ruane; and M.K. Van Ittersum. 2015. Exploring climate change impacts and adaptation options for maize production in the Central Rift Valley of Ethiopia using different climate change scenarios and crop models. *Climatic Change* **129:145–158**.

Khatri-Chhetri, A.; P.K. Aggarwal; P.K. Joshi; and S. Vyas. 2017. Farmers' prioritization of climate-smart agriculture (CSA) technologies. *Agricultural Systems* **151:184–191**.

Khatri-Chhetri, A.; A. Pant; P.K. Aggarwal; V.V. Vasireddy; and A. Yadav. 2019. Stakeholders prioritization of climate-smart agriculture interventions: Evaluation of a framework. *Agricultural Systems* **174:23–31**.

Kibuka-Musoke, D. 2007. Issue paper II: OECD, African Partnership Forum.

Kim, H.Y.; J. Ko; S. Kang; and J. Tenhunen. 2013. Impacts of climate change on paddy rice yield in a temperate climate. *Global Change Biology* **19:548–562**.

Kogo, B.K.; L. Kumar; and R. Koech. 2021. Climate change and variability in Kenya: A review of impacts on agriculture and food security. *Environment, Development and Sustainability* **23:23–43**.

Kombat, R.; P. Sarfatti; and O.A. Fatunbi. 2021. A review of climate-smart agriculture technology adoption by farming households in Sub-Saharan Africa. *Sustainability* **13:12130**.

Kongsager, R. 2017. Barriers to the adoption of alley cropping as a climate-smart agriculture practice: Lessons from maize cultivation among the Maya in southern Belize. *Forests* **8:260**.

Koutroulis, A.; L. Papadimitriou; M. Grillakis; I. Tsanis; R. Warren; and R. Betts. 2019. Global water availability under high-end climate change: A vulnerability based assessment. *Global and Planetary Change* **175:52–63**.

Kumar, R.; M. Patra; A. Thirugnanavel; B.C. Deka; D. Chatterjee; T. Borah; G. Rajesha; H. Talang; S. Ray; and M. Kumar. 2018. Comparative evaluation of different integrated farming system models for small and marginal farmers under the Eastern Himalayas. *Indian Journal of Agricultural Sciences* **88:1722–1729**.

Kumar, V.; P. Rajput; and A. Goel. 2018. Atmospheric abundance of HULIS during wintertime in Indo-Gangetic Plain: Impact of biomass burning emissions. *Journal of Atmospheric Chemistry* **75:385–398**.

Lam, V.W.; W.W. Cheung; G. Reygondeau; and U.R. Sumaila. 2016. Projected change in global fisheries revenues under climate change. *Scientific Reports* **6:1–8**.

Lammers, K.; P. Bertheau; and P. Blechinger. 2020. Exploring requirements for sustainable energy supply planning with regard to climate resilience of Southeast Asian islands. *Energy Policy* **146:111770**.

Leal Filho, W.; U.M. Azeiteiro; A.-L. Balogun; A.F.F. Setti; S.A. Mucova; D. Ayal; E. Totin; A.M. Lydia; F.K. Kalaba; and N.O. Oguge. 2021. The influence of ecosystems services depletion to climate change adaptation efforts in Africa. *Science of The Total Environment*:**146414**.

Lesage, D. and T. Van de Graaf. 2016. *Global energy governance in a multipolar world*. Routledge.

Lidwell-Durnin, J. and A. Lapthorn. 2020. The threat to global food security from wheat rust: Ethical and historical issues in fighting crop diseases and preserving genetic diversity. *Global Food Security* **26:100446**.

Lipper, L.; N. McCarthy; D. Zilberman; S. Asfaw; and G. Branca. 2017. *Climate smart agriculture: Building resilience to climate change*. Springer Nature.

Lipper, L. and D. Zilberman. 2018. A short history of the evolution of the climate smart agriculture approach and its links to climate change and sustainable agriculture debates. In *Climate smart agriculture*, 13–30: Springer, Cham.

Lobell, D.B. and S.M. Gourdji. 2012. The influence of climate change on global crop productivity. *Plant physiology* **160:1686–1697**.

Lu, S.; X. Bai; W. Li; and N. Wang. 2019. Impacts of climate change on water resources and grain production. *Technological Forecasting and Social Change* **143:76–84**.

Ludwig, M.; P. Wilmes; and S. Schrader. 2018. Measuring soil sustainability via soil resilience. *Science of The Total Environment* **626:1484–1493**.

Luthra, S.; S. Kumar; R. Kharb; M.F. Ansari; and S. Shimmi. 2014. Adoption of smart grid technologies: An analysis of interactions among barriers. *Renewable and Sustainable Energy Reviews* **33:554–565**.

Lynch, D.H. 2015. Nutrient cycling and soil health in organic cropping systems-importance of management strategies and soil resilience. *Sustainable Agriculture Research* **4**.

Ma, L.; Q. Fang; M. Sima; K. Burkey; and R. Harmel. 2021. Simulated climate change effects on soybean production using two crop modules in RZWQM2. *Agronomy Journal* **113:1349–1365**.

Mahato, A. 2014. Climate change and its impact on agriculture. *International Journal of Scientific and Research Publications* **4:1–6**.

Malhi, G.S.; M. Kaur; and P. Kaushik. 2021. Impact of climate change on agriculture and its mitigation strategies: A review. *Sustainability* **13:1318**.

Mall, R.; N. Singh; K. Singh; G. Sonkar; and A. Gupta. 2018. Evaluating the performance of RegCM4. 0 climate model for climate change impact assessment on wheat and rice crop in diverse agro-climatic zones of Uttar Pradesh, India. *Climatic Change* **149:503–515**.

Mall, R.K.; A. Gupta; and G. Sonkar. 2017. Effect of climate change on agricultural crops. In *Current developments in biotechnology and bioengineering*, 23–46: Elsevier.

Martinho, V.J.P.D. and R.d.P.F. Guiné. 2021. Integrated-smart agriculture: Contexts and assumptions for a broader concept. *Agronomy* **11:1568**.

Masud, M.M.; M.N. Azam; M. Mohiuddin; H. Banna; R. Akhtar; A.F. Alam; and H. Begum. 2017. Adaptation barriers and strategies towards climate change: Challenges in the agricultural sector. *Journal of Cleaner Production* **156:698–706**.

Mbuli, C.S.; L.N. Fonjong; and A.J. Fletcher. 2021. Climate change and small farmers' vulnerability to food insecurity in cameroon. *Sustainability* **13:1523**.

Moebius-Clune, B. 2017. Soil health initiatives of the USDA Natural Resources Conservation Service (NRCS).

Morkunas, M. and T. Balezentis. 2021. Is agricultural revitalization possible through the climate-smart agriculture: A systematic review and citation-based analysis. *Management of Environmental Quality: An International Journal.*

Moss, E.D.; D.M. Evans; and J.P. Atkins. 2021. Investigating the impacts of climate change on ecosystem services in UK agro-ecosystems: An application of the DPSIR framework. *Land Use Policy* **105:105394**.

Mukherjee, A.K. and K. Batabyal. 2021. Climate-smart soil management: Prospect and challenges in Indian Scenario. In *Soil science: Fundamentals to recent advances*, 875–902: Springer.

Mulungu, K. and J.N. Ng'ombe. 2019. Climate change impacts on sustainable maize production in Sub-Saharan Africa: A review. *Maize Prod. Use.*

Mwongera, C.; K.M. Shikuku; J. Twyman; P. Läderach; E. Ampaire; P. Van Asten; S. Twomlow; and L.A. Winowiecki. 2017. Climate smart agriculture rapid appraisal (CSA-RA): A tool for prioritizing context-specific climate smart agriculture technologies. *Agricultural Systems* **151:192–203**.

Nakicenovic, N. and R. Swart. 2000. Emissions scenarios-special report of the Intergovernmental Panel on Climate Change.

Nayak, A.; S. Mohanty; D. Chatterjee; D. Bhaduri; R. Khanam; M. Shahid; R. Tripathi; A. Kumar; S. Munda; and U. Kumar. 2018. Nutrient management for enhancing productivity and nutrient use efficiency in rice: ICAR-NRRI.

Nguyen, T.-H.; O. Sahin; and M. Howes. 2021. Climate change adaptation influences and barriers impacting the asian agricultural industry. *Sustainability* **13:7346**.

Noll, B.; T. Filatova; and A. Need. 2020. How does private adaptation motivation to climate change vary across cultures? Evidence from a meta-analysis. *International Journal of Disaster Risk Reduction* **46:101615**.

OECD. 2014. Stimulation demand for innovation. OECD, Paris, France.

Olayide, O.E.; I.K. Tetteh; and L. Popoola. 2016. Differential impacts of rainfall and irrigation on agricultural production in Nigeria: Any lessons for climate-smart agriculture? *Agricultural Water Management* **178:30–36**.

Olesen, J.E.; M. Trnka; K.C. Kersebaum; A.O. Skjelvåg; B. Seguin; P. Peltonen-Sainio; F. Rossi; J. Kozyra; and F. Micale. 2011. Impacts and adaptation of European crop production systems to climate change. *European Journal of Agronomy* **34:96–112**.

Olhoff, A. and J. Christensen. 2017. Scoping the emissions gap report 2017—The Emissions Gap Report 2017 Chapter 1. *The Emissions Gap Report 2017: A UN Environment Synthesis Report*.

Oyebola, O.O. and O.M. Olatunde. 2019. Climate change adaptation through aquaculture: Ecological considerations and regulatory requirements for tropical Africa. In *Agriculture and s Sub Saharan Africa*, 435–472: Springer.

Paudel, B.; R.C. Khanal; A. KC; K. Bhatta; and P. Chaudhary. 2017. Climate-smart agriculture in Nepal. *Research program on climate change, agriculture and food security*.

Paz-Ferreiro, J. and S. Fu. 2016. Biological indices for soil quality evaluation: Perspectives and limitations. *Land Degradation & Development* **27:14–25**.

Perkins, J.H. 2012. Special report on renewable energy sources and climate change mitigation: 2011. Intergovernmental Panel on Climate Change, Working Group III—Mitigation of Climate Change. Cambridge University Press, Cambridge, England. 1088 pp. $100.00 hardcover (ISBN13: 9781107607101). Also available for free at http://srren.ipcc-wg3.de/report (ca. 1544 pp.): Taylor & Francis.

Pierce, F.J. and W. Larson. 1993. Developing criteria to evaluate sustainable land management. In *Proceedings of the eighth international soil management workshop: Utilization of soil survey information for sustainable land use*, 7–14: US Dept. Agr., Soil Cons. Serv., Lincoln, NE. May.

Plagányi, É. 2019. Climate change impacts on fisheries. *Science* **363:930–931**.

Ponisio, L.C.; L.K. M'Gonigle; K.C. Mace; J. Palomino; P. De Valpine; and C. Kremen. 2015. Diversification practices reduce organic to conventional yield gap. *Proceedings of the Royal Society B: Biological Sciences* **282:20141396**.

Prasad, Y.; C.S. Rao; J. Prasad; K. Rao; D. Ramana; K. Gopinath; I. Srinivas; B.S. Reddy; R. Adake; and V. Rao. 2015. *Technology demonstrations-enhancing resilience and adaptive capacity of farmers to climate variability*. Not Available.

Prestele, R. and P.H. Verburg. 2020. The overlooked spatial dimension of climate-smart agriculture. *Global Change Biology* **26:1045–1054**.

Radovanović, M.; S. Filipović; and D. Pavlović. 2017. Energy security measurement—A sustainable approach. *Renewable and Sustainable Energy Reviews* **68:1020–1032**.

Rahman, H. and G.M. Hickey. 2020. An analytical framework for assessing context-specific rural livelihood vulnerability. *Sustainability* **12:5654**.

Raiesi, F. 2017. A minimum data set and soil quality index to quantify the effect of land use conversion on soil quality and degradation in native rangelands of upland arid and semiarid regions. *Ecological Indicators* **75:307–320**.

Rockström, J.; J. Williams; G. Daily; A. Noble; N. Matthews; L. Gordon; H. Wetterstrand; F. DeClerck; M. Shah; and P. Steduto. 2017. Sustainable intensification of agriculture for human prosperity and global sustainability. *Ambio* **46:4–17**.

Ruane, A.C.; L.D. Cecil; R.M. Horton; R. Gordón; R. McCollum; D. Brown; B. Killough; R. Goldberg; A.P. Greeley; and C. Rosenzweig. 2013. Climate change impact uncertainties for maize in Panama: Farm information, climate projections, and yield sensitivities. *Agricultural and Forest Meteorology* **170:132–145**.

Rubio-Asensio, J.S. and A.J. Bloom. 2017. Inorganic nitrogen form: A major player in wheat and Arabidopsis responses to elevated CO_2. *Journal of Experimental Botany* **68:2611–2625**.

Salomé, C.; P. Coll; E. Lardo; A. Metay; C. Villenave; C. Marsden; E. Blanchart; P. Hinsinger; and E. Le Cadre. 2016. The soil quality concept as a framework to assess management practices in vulnerable agroecosystems: A case study in Mediterranean vineyards. *Ecological Indicators* **61:456–465**.

Sarkodie, S.A.; S. Adams; and T. Leirvik. 2020. Foreign direct investment and renewable energy in climate change mitigation: does governance matter? *Journal of Cleaner Production* **263:121262**.

Schilling, J.; E. Hertig; Y. Tramblay; and J. Scheffran. 2020. Climate change vulnerability, water resources and social implications in North Africa. *Regional Environmental Change* **20:1–12**.

Schlenker, W. and D.B. Lobell. 2010. Robust negative impacts of climate change on African agriculture. *Environmental Research Letters* **5:014010**.

Seybold, C.; M. Mansbach; D. Karlen; and H. Rogers. 2018. Quantification of soil quality. In *Soil processes and the carbon cycle*, 387–404: CRC Press.

Sikka, A.K.; A. Islam; and K. Rao. 2018. Climate-smart land and water management for sustainable agriculture. *Irrigation and Drainage* **67:72–81**.

Sofi, I.A.; I. Rashid; J.Y. Lone; S. Tyagi; Z.A. Reshi; and R.R. Mir. 2021. Genetic diversity may help evolutionary rescue in a clonal endemic plant species of Western Himalaya. *Scientific Reports* **11:1–15**.

Southworth, J.; J. Randolph; M. Habeck; O. Doering; R. Pfeifer; D.G. Rao; and J. Johnston. 2000. Consequences of future climate change and changing climate variability on maize yields in the midwestern United States. *Agriculture, Ecosystems & Environment* **82:139–158**.

Staudinger, M.D.; N.B. Grimm; A. Staudt; S.L. Carter; and F.S. Chapin. 2012. Impacts of climate change on biodiversity, ecosystems, and ecosystem services. *United States Global Change Research Program, Washington, DC.*

Stoerk, T.; G. Wagner; and R.E. Ward. 2020. Policy brief—Recommendations for improving the treatment of risk and uncertainty in economic estimates of climate impacts in the sixth Intergovernmental Panel on Climate Change assessment report. *Review of Environmental Economics and Policy.*

Streimikis, J.; Z. Miao; and T. Balezentis. 2021. Creation of climate-smart and energy-efficient agriculture in the European Union: Pathways based on the frontier analysis. *Business Strategy and the Environment* **30:576–589**.

Stuart, C. and S. Escudero. 2017. Energy and climate change adaptation in developing countries. *European Union Energy Initiative Partnership Dialogue Facility (EUEI PDF).*

Summit, U.C. 2014. New York declaration on forests. *United Nations, New York, NY.*

Sun, S.; Y. Wang; F. Wang; J. Liu; X. Luan; X. Li; T. Zhou; and P. Wu. 2015. Alleviating pressure on water resources: A new approach could be attempted. *Scientific Reports* **5:1–12**.

Taneja, G.; B.D. Pal; P.K. Joshi; P.K. Aggarwal; and N.K. Tyagi. 2019. Farmers' preferences for climate-smart agriculture—An assessment in the Indo-Gangetic Plain. In *Climate smart agriculture in South Asia*, 91–111: Springer.

Tankha, S.; D. Fernandes; and N. Narayanan. 2020. Overcoming barriers to climate smart agriculture in India. *International Journal of Climate Change Strategies and Management.*

Taylor, M. 2018. Climate-smart agriculture: What is it good for? *The Journal of Peasant Studies* **45:89–107**.

Teixeira, E.I.; G. Fischer; H. Van Velthuizen; C. Walter; and F. Ewert. 2013. Global hot-spots of heat stress on agricultural crops due to climate change. *Agricultural and forest Meteorology* **170:206–215**.

Thoumazeau, A.; C. Bessou; M.-S. Renevier; J. Trap; R. Marichal; L. Mareschal; T. Decaëns; N. Bottinelli; B. Jaillard; and T. Chevallier. 2019. Biofunctool®: A new framework to assess the impact of land management on soil quality. Part A: Concept and validation of the set of indicators. *Ecological Indicators* **97:100–110**.

Totin, E.; A.C. Segnon; M. Schut; H. Affognon; R.B. Zougmoré; T. Rosenstock; and P.K. Thornton. 2018. Institutional perspectives of climate-smart agriculture: A systematic literature review. *Sustainability* **10:1990**.

Trnka, M.; R.P. Rötter; M. Ruiz-Ramos; K.C. Kersebaum; J.E. Olesen; Z. Žalud; and M.A. Semenov. 2014. Adverse weather conditions for European wheat production will become more frequent with climate change. *Nature Climate Change* **4:637–643**.

Tsige, M.; G. Synnevåg; and J.B. Aune. 2020. Gendered constraints for adopting climate-smart agriculture amongst smallholder Ethiopian women farmers. *Scientific African* **7:e00250**.

Venkatramanan, V.; S. Shah; and R. Prasad. 2020. *Global climate change: Resilient and smart agriculture*. Springer.

Vijayalakshmi, D. and M.D. Barbhai. 2021. Resilient measures in face of climate change to strengthen food and nutritional security. In *Climate change and resilient food systems*, 113–140: Springer.

Wang, L.; Z. Feng; and J.K. Schjoerring. 2013. Effects of elevated atmospheric CO2 on physiology and yield of wheat (Triticum aestivum L.): A meta-analytic test of current hypotheses. *Agriculture, Ecosystems & Environment* **178:57–63**.

Ward, P.S.; A.R. Bell; K. Droppelmann; and T.G. Benton. 2018. Early adoption of conservation agriculture practices: Understanding partial compliance in programs with multiple adoption decisions. *Land Use Policy* **70:27–37**.

Wassmann, R.; J. Villanueva; M. Khounthavong; B.O. Okumu; T.B.T. Vo; and B.O. Sander. 2019. Adaptation, mitigation and food security: Multi-criteria ranking system for climate-smart agriculture technologies illustrated for rainfed rice in Laos. *Global Food Security* **23:33–40**.

Weiskopf, S.R.; M.A. Rubenstein; L.G. Crozier; S. Gaichas; R. Griffis; J.E. Halofsky; K.J. Hyde; T.L. Morelli; J.T. Morisette; and R.C. Muñoz. 2020. Climate change effects on biodiversity, ecosystems, ecosystem services, and natural resource management in the United States. *Science of The Total Environment* **733:137782**.

Westermann, O.; W. Förch; P. Thornton; J. Körner; L. Cramer; and B. Campbell. 2018. Scaling up agricultural interventions: Case studies of climate-smart agriculture. *Agricultural Systems* **165:283–293**.

Winkelman, S.; E. Nichol; and D. Harford. 2017. Taking action on green resilience: Climate change adaptation and mitigation synergies.

Wubben, E.; N. Runge; and V. Blok. 2012. From waste to profit: An interorganisational perspective on drivers for biomass valorisation. *Journal on Chain and Network Science* **12:261–272**.

Yadav, A.; A. Bhatia; S. Yadav; V. Kumar; and B. Singh. 2019. The effects of elevated CO2 and elevated O3 exposure on plant growth, yield and quality of grains of two wheat cultivars grown in north India. *Heliyon* **5:e02317**.

Zach, A.; H. Tiessen; and E. Noellemeyer. 2006. Carbon turnover and carbon-13 natural abundance under land use change in semiarid savanna soils of La Pampa, Argentina. *Soil Science Society of America Journal* **70:1541–1546**.

Zhao, C.; B. Liu; S. Piao; X. Wang; D.B. Lobell; Y. Huang; M. Huang; Y. Yao; S. Bassu; and P. Ciais. 2017. Temperature increase reduces global yields of major crops in four independent estimates. *Proceedings of the National Academy of Sciences* **114:9326–9331**.

Zhou, M. and H. Wang. 2015. Potential impact of future climate change on crop yield in northeastern China. *Advances in Atmospheric Sciences* **32:889–897**.

Index

M. Coromaldi and S. Auci (eds.), *Climate-Induced Innovation*,
https://doi.org/10.1007/978-3-031-01330-0

The manufacturer's authorised representative in the EU is Springer Nature Customer Service Centre GmbH, Europaplatz 3, 69115 Heidelberg, Germany. If you have any concerns regarding our products, please contact ProductSafety@springernature.com

Printed and bound by CPI Group (UK) Ltd, Croydon, CR0 4YY
30/09/2026
02225260-0013